CRUSADERS OF NEW FRANCE

THE YALE CHRONICLES
OF AMERICA SERIES

Crusaders
of
New France

A Chronicle of
the Fleur-de-lis
in the Wilderness

by
William B. Munro

1974
Toronto
Glasgow, Brook & Co.

New York
United States Publishers
Association, Inc.

To

my good friend

FATHER HENRI BEAUDÉ
(*Henri d'Arles*)

this tribute to the men
of his race and faith is
affectionately inscribed.

CONTENTS

CRUSADERS OF NEW FRANCE

∴

CHAPTER I

FRANCE OF THE BOURBONS

FRANCE, when she undertook the creation of a
Bourbon empire beyond the seas, was the first
nation of Europe. Her population was larger
than that of Spain, and three times that of England. Her army in the days of Louis Quatorze,
numbering nearly a half-million in all ranks, was
larger than that of Rome at the height of the
imperial power. No nation since the fall of
Roman supremacy had possessed such resources
for conquering and colonizing new lands. By
the middle of the seventeenth century Spain
had ceased to be a dangerous rival; Germany and
Italy were at the time little more than geographical expressions, while England was in the throes
of the Puritan Revolution.

Nor was it only in the arts of war that the hegemony of the Bourbon kingdom stood unquestioned. In art and education, in manners and fashions, France also dominated the ideas of the old continent, the dictator of social tastes as well as the grim warrior among the nations. In the second half of the seventeenth century France might justly claim to be both the heart and the head of Europe. Small wonder it was that the leaders of such a nation should demand to see the "clause in Adam's will" which bequeathed the New World to Spain and Portugal. Small wonder, indeed, that the first nation of Europe should insist upon a place in the sun to which her people might go to trade, to make land yield its increase, and to widen the Bourbon sway. If ever there was a land able and ready to take up the white man's burden, it was the France of Louis XIV.

The power and prestige of France at this time may be traced, in the main, to three sources. First there were the physical features, the compactness of the kingdom, a fertile soil, a propitious climate, and a frontage upon two great seas. In an age when so much of a nation's wealth came from agriculture these were factors of great importance. Only in commerce did the French people at this time find themselves outstripped by their neighbors. Although both the Atlantic and the Mediterranean bathed the shores of France, her people were being outdistanced on the seas by the English and the Dutch, whose commercial companies were exploiting the wealth of the new continents both east and west. Yet in France there was food enough for all and to spare; it was only because the means of distributing it were so poor that some got more and others less than they required. France was supporting at this time a population half as large as that of two centuries later.

Then there were qualities of race which helped to make the nation great. At all periods in their history the French have shown an almost inexhaustible stamina, an ability to bear disasters, and to rise from them quickly, a courage and persistence that no obstacles seem able to thwart. How often in the course of the centuries has France been torn apart by internecine strife or thrown prostrate by her enemies only to astonish the world by a superb display of recuperative powers! It was France that first among the kingdoms of Europe rose from feudal chaos to orderly nationalism; it was France that first among

continental countries after the Middle Ages
established the reign of law throughout a powerful realm. Though wars and turmoils almost
without end were a heavy drain upon Gallic
vitality for many generations, France achieved
steady progress to primacy in the arts of peace.
None but a marvellous people could have made
such efforts without exhaustion, yet even now
in the twentieth century the astounding vigor
of this race has not ceased to compel the admiration of mankind.

In the seventeenth century, moreover, France
owed much of her national power to a highly-cen-
tralized and closely-knit scheme of government.
Under Richelieu the strength of the monarchy
had been enhanced and the power of the nobility
broken. When he began his personal rule, Louis
XIV continued his work of consolidation and in
the years of his long reign managed to centralize
in the throne every vestige of political power.
The famous saying attributed to him, "The
State! I am the State!" embodied no idle boast.
Nowhere was there a trace of representative
government, nowhere a constitutional check on
the royal power. There were councils of different
sorts and with varied jurisdictions, but men sat in

them at the King's behest and were removable at his will. There were *parlements*, too, but to mention them without explanation would be only to let the term mislead, for they were not representative bodies or parliaments in the ordinary sense: their powers were chiefly judicial and they were no barrier in the way of the steady march to absolutism. The political structure of the Bourbon realm in the age of Louis XIV and afterwards was simple: all the lines of control ran upwards and to a common center. And all this made for unity and autocratic efficiency in finance, in war, and in foreign affairs.

Another feature which fitted the nation for an imperial destiny was the possession of a united and militant church. With heresy the Gallican branch of the Catholic Church had fought a fierce struggle, but, before the seventeenth century was far advanced, the battle had been won. There were heretics in France even after Richelieu's time, but they were no longer a source of serious discord. The Church, now victorious over its foes, became militant, ready to carry its missionary efforts to other lands — ready, in fact, for a new crusade.

These four factors, rare geographical advantages, racial qualities of a high order, a strongly centralized scheme of government, and a militant church, contributed largely to the prestige which France possessed among European nations in the seventeenth century. With all these advantages she should have been the first and not the last to get a firm footing in the new continents. Historians have recorded their reasons why France did not seriously enter the field of American colonization as early as England, but these reasons do not impress one as being good. Foreign wars and internal religious strife are commonly given and accepted as the true cause of French tardiness in following up the pioneer work of Jacques Cartier and others. Yet not all the energy of nearly twenty million people was being absorbed in these troubles. There were men and money to spare, had the importance of the work overseas only been adequately realized.

The main reason why France was last in the field is to be found in the failure of her kings and ministers to realize until late in the day how vast the possibilities of the new continent really were. In a highly centralized and not over-populated state the authorities must lead the way in colonial enterprises; the people will not of their own initiative seek out and follow opportunities to colonize distant lands. And in France the authorities were not ready to lead. Sully, who stood supreme among the royal advisers in the closing years of the sixteenth century, was opposed to colonial ventures under all circumstances. "Far-off possessions," he declared, "are not suited to the temperament or to the genius of Frenchmen, who to my great regret have neither the perseverance nor the foresight needed for such enterprises, but who ordinarily apply their vigor, minds, and courage to things which are immediately at hand and constantly before their eyes." Colonies beyond the seas, he believed, "would never be anything but a great expense." That, indeed, was the orthodox notion in circles surrounding the seat of royal power, and it was a difficult notion to dislodge.

Never until the time of Richelieu was any intimation of the great colonial opportunity, now quickly slipping by, allowed to reach the throne, and then it was only an inkling, making but a slight impression and soon virtually forgotten. Richelieu's great Company of 1627 made a brave start, but it did not hold the Cardinal's interest very long. Mazarin, who succeeded Richelieu, took no interest in the New World; the tortuous problems of European diplomacy appealed far more strongly to his Italian imagination than did the vision of a New France beyond the seas. It was not until Colbert took the reins that official France really displayed an interest in the work of colonization at all proportionate to the nation's power and resources.

Colbert was admirably fitted to become the herald of a greater France. Coming from the ranks of the *bourgeoisie*, he was a man of affairs, not a cleric or a courtier as his predecessors in office had been. He had a clear conception of what he wanted and unwearied industry in moving towards the desired end. His devotion to the King was beyond question; he had native ability, patience, sound ideas, and a firm will. Given a fair opportunity, he would have accomplished far more for the glory of the fleur-de-lis in the region of the St. Lawrence and the Great Lakes of America. But a thousand problems of home administration were crowded upon him, problems of finance, of industry, of ecclesiastical adjustment, and of social reconstruction. In the first few years of his term as minister he could still find a little time and thought for Canada, and during this short period he personally conducted the corre-

spondence with the colonial officials; but after 1669
all this was turned over to the Minister of Marine,
and Colbert himself figured directly in the affairs
of the colony no more.   The great minister of
Louis XIV is remembered far more for his work
at home than for his services to New France.

As for the French monarchs of the seventeenth
century, Louis XIV was the first and only one to
take an active and enduring interest in the great
crusade to the northern wilderness.   He began his
personal reign about 1660 with a genuine display
of zeal for the establishment of a colony which
would by its rapid growth and prosperity soon
crowd the English off the new continent.   In the
selection of officials to carry out his policy, his
judgment, when not subjected to sinister pressure,
was excellent, as shown in his choice of Frontenac.
Nor did the King's interest in the colony slacken
in the face of discouragement.   It kept on to the
end of his reign, although diminishing somewhat
towards the close.   It could not well do otherwise
than weaken during the European disasters which
marked his later years.   By the death of Louis XIV
in 1715 the colony lost its most unwavering friend.

The shrewdest of French historians, De Tocque-
ville, has somewhere remarked that "the physi-

ognomy of a government may be best judged in the colonies. . . . When I wish to study the spirit and faults of the administration of Louis XIV," he writes, "I must go to Canada, for its deformity is there seen as through a microscope." That is entirely true. The history of New France in its picturesque alternation of sunshine and shadow, of victory and defeat, of pageant and tragedy, is a chronicle that is Gallic to the core. In the early annals of the northland one can find silhouetted in sharp relief examples of all that was best and all that was worst in the life of Old France. The political framework of the colony, with its strict centralization, the paternal regulation of industry and commerce, the flood of missionary zeal which poured in upon it, the heroism and courage of its priests and voyageurs, the venality of its administrative officials, the anachronism of a feudal land-tenure, the bizarre externals of its social life, the versatility of its people — all these reflected the paternity of New France.

The most striking weakness of French colonial policy in the seventeenth century was its failure to realize how vastly different was the environment of North America from that of Central Europe. Institutions were transplanted bodily, and then amazement was expressed at Versailles because they did not seem to thrive in the new soil. Detailed instructions to officials in New France were framed by men who had not the slightest grasp of the colony's needs or problems. One busybody wrote to the colonial Intendant that a bake-oven should be established in every seigneury and that the *habitants* should be ordered to bring their dough there to be made into bread. The Intendant had to remind him that, in the long cold winters of the St. Lawrence valley, the dough would be frozen stiff if the habitants, with their dwellings so widely scattered, were required to do anything of the kind. Another martinet gravely informed the colonial authorities that, as a protection against Indian attacks "all the seigneuries should be palisaded." And some of the seigneurial estates were eight or ten miles square! The dogmatic way in which the colonial officials were told to do this and that, to encourage one thing and to discourage another, all by superiors who displayed an astounding ignorance of New World conditions, must have been a severe trial to the patience of those hard-working officials who were never without great practical difficulties immediately before their eyes.

Not enough heed was paid, moreover, to the advice of men who were on the spot. It is true that the recommendations sent home to France by the Governor and by the Intendant were often contradictory, but even where the two officials were agreed there was no certainty that their counsel would be taken. With greater freedom and discretion the colonial government could have accomplished much more in the way of developing trade and industry; but for every step the acquiescence of the home authorities had first to be secured. To obtain this consent always entailed a great loss of time, and when the approval arrived the opportunity too often had passed. From November until May there was absolutely no communication between Quebec and Paris save that in a great emergency, if France and England happened to be at peace, a dispatch might be sent by dint of great hardship to Boston with a precarious chance that it would get across to the French ambassador in London. Ordinarily the officials sent their requests for instructions by the homegoing vessels from Quebec in the autumn and received their answers by the ships which came in the following spring. If any plans were formulated after the last ship sailed in October, it ordinarily took eighteen months before the royal approval could be had for putting them into effect. The routine machinery of paternalism thus ran with exasperating slowness.

There was, however, one mitigating feature in the situation. The hand of home authority was rigid and its beckonings were precise; but as a practical matter it could be, and sometimes was, disregarded altogether. Not that the colonial officials ever defied the King or his ministers, or ever failed to profess their intent to follow the royal instructions loyally and to the letter. They had a much safer plan. When the provisions of a royal decree seemed impractical or unwise, it was easy enough to let them stand unenforced. Such decrees were duly registered in the records of the Sovereign Council at Quebec and were then promptly pigeonholed so that no one outside the little circle of officials at the Château de St. Louis ever heard of them. In one case a new intendant on coming to the colony unearthed a royal mandate of great importance which had been kept from public knowledge for twenty years.

Absolutism, paternalism, and religious solidarity were characteristic of both France and her colonies in the great century of overseas expansion. There was no self-government, no freedom of individual initiative, and very little heresy either at home or abroad. The factors which made France strong in Europe, her unity, her subordination of all other things to the military needs of the nation, her fostering of the sense of nationalism — these appeared prominently in Canada and helped to make the colony strong as well. Historians of New France have been at pains to explain why the colony ultimately succumbed to the combined attacks of New England by land and of Old England by sea. For a full century New France had as its next-door neighbor a group of English colonies whose combined populations outnumbered her own at a ratio of about fifteen to one. The relative numbers and resources of the two areas were about the same, proportionately, as those of the United States and Canada at the present day. The marvel is not that French dominion in America finally came to an end but that it managed to endure so long.

CHAPTER II

THE closing quarter of the fifteenth century in Europe has usually been regarded by historians as marking the end of the Middle Ages. The era of feudal chaos had drawn to a close and states were being welded together under the leadership of strong dynasties. With this consolidation came the desire for expansion, for acquiring new lands, and for opening up new channels of influence. Spain, Portugal, and England were first in the field of active exploration, searching for stores of precious metals and for new routes to the coasts of Ormuz and of India. In this quest for a short route to the half-fabulous empires of Asia they had literally stumbled upon a new continent which they had made haste to exploit. France, meanwhile, was dissipating her energies on Spanish and Italian battlefields. It was not until the peace of Cambrai in 1529 ended the struggle with

Spain that France gave any attention to the work of gaining some foothold in the New World. By that time Spain had become firmly entrenched in the lands which border the Caribbean Sea; her galleons were already bearing home their rich cargoes of silver bullion. Portugal, England, and even Holland had already turned with zeal to the exploration of new lands in the East and the West; French fishermen, it is true, were lengthening their voyages to the west; every year now the rugged old Norman and Breton seaports were sending their fleets of small vessels to gather the harvests of the sea. But official France took no active interest in the regions toward which they went.

Five years after the peace of Cambrai the Breton port of St. Malo became the starting point of the first French voyageur to the St. Lawrence. Francis I had been persuaded to turn his thoughts from gaming and gallantries to the trading prospects of his kingdom, with the result that in 1534 Jacques Cartier was able to set out on his first voyage of discovery. Cartier is described in the records of the time as a corsair—which means that he had made a business of roving the seas to despoil the enemies of France. St. Malo, his birthplace and home, on the coast of Brittany, faces the English Channel somewhat south of Jersey, the nearest of the Channel Islands. The town is set on high ground which projects out into the sea, forming an almost landlocked harbor where ships may ride at ease during the most tumultuous gales. It had long been a notable nursery of hardy fishermen and adventurous navigators, men who had pressed their way to all the coasts of Europe and beyond.

Cartier was one of these hardy sailors. His fathers before him had been mariners, and he had himself learned the way of the great waters while yet a mere youth. Before his expedition of 1534 Jacques Cartier had probably made a voyage to Brazil and had in all probability more than once visited the Newfoundland fishing-banks. Although, when he sailed from St. Malo to become the pathfinder of a new Bourbon imperialism, he was forty-three years of age and in the prime of his days, we know very little of his youth and early manhood. It is enough that he had attained the rank of a master-pilot and that, from his skill in seamanship, he was considered the most dependable man in all the kingdom to serve his august sovereign in this important enterprise.

Cartier shipped his crew at St. Malo, and on the

20th of April, 1534, headed his two small ships
across the great Atlantic. His company numbered
only threescore souls in all. Favored by steady
winds his vessels made good progress, and within
three weeks he sighted the shores of Newfoundland where he put into one of the many small
harbors to rest and refit his ships. Then, turning
northward, the expedition passed through the
straits of Belle Isle and into the Gulf of St. Lawrence. Coasting along the northern shore of
the Gulf for a short distance, Cartier headed his
ships due southward, keeping close to the western
shore of the great island almost its whole length;
he then struck across the lower Gulf and, moving northward once more, reached the Baie des
Chaleurs on the 6th July. Here the boats were sent
ashore and the French were able to do a little trading with the Indians. About a week later, Cartier
went northward once more and soon sought shelter
from a violent gulf storm by anchoring in Gaspé
Bay. On the headland there he planted a great
wooden cross with the arms of France, the first
symbol of Bourbon dominion in the New Land,
and the same symbol that successive explorers,
chanting the *Vexilla Regis*, were in time to set aloft
from the Gulf of St. Lawrence to the Gulf of

Mexico. It was the augury of the white man's coming.

Crossing next to the southerly shore of Anticosti the voyageurs almost circled the island until the constant and adverse winds which Cartier met in the gradually narrowing channel forced him to defer indefinitely his hope of finding a western passage, and he therefore headed his ships back to Belle Isle. It was now mid-August, and the season of autumnal storms was drawing near. Cartier had come to explore, to search for a westward route to the Indies, to look for precious metals, not to establish a colony. He accordingly decided to set sail for home and, with favoring winds, was able to reach St. Malo in the early days of September.

In one sense the voyage of 1534 had been a failure. No stores of mineral wealth had been discovered and no short route to Cipango or Cathay. Yet the spirit of exploration had been awakened. Cartier's recital of his voyage had aroused the interest of both the King and his people, so that the navigator's request for better equipment to make another voyage was readily granted. On May 19, 1535, Cartier once more set forth from St. Malo, this time with three vessels and with a royal patent empowering him to take possession of new lands in his sovereign's name. With Cartier on this voyage there were over one hundred men, of whom the majority were hardened Malouins, veterans of the sea. How he found accommodation for all of them, with supplies and provisions, in three small vessels whose total burden was only two hundred and twenty tons, is not least among the mysteries of this remarkable voyage.[1]

The trip across the ocean was boisterous, and the clumsy caravels had a hard time breasting the waves. The ships were soon separated by alternate storms and fog so that all three did not meet at their appointed rendezvous in the Straits of Belle Isle until the last week in July. Then moving westward along the north shore of the Gulf, they passed Anticosti, crossed to the Gaspé shore, circled back as far as the Mingan islands, and then resumed a westward course up the great river. As the vessels stemmed the current but

[1] The shipbuilders' old measure for determining tonnage was to multiply the length of a vessel minus three-quarters of the beam by the beam, then to multiply the product by one-half the beam, then to divide this final product by 94. The resulting quotient was the tonnage. On this basis Cartier's three ships were 67 feet length by 23 feet beam, 57 feet length by 17 feet beam, and 48 feet length by 17 feet beam, respectively.

slowly, it was well into September when they cast anchor before the Indian village of Stadacona which occupied the present site of Lower Quebec.

Since it was now too late in the season to think of returning at once to France, Cartier decided to spend the winter at this point. Two of the ships were therefore drawn into the mouth of a brook which entered the river just below the village, while the Frenchmen established acquaintance with the Indians and made preparations for a trip farther up the river in the smallest vessel. Using as interpreters two young Indians whom he had captured in the Gaspé region during his first voyage in the preceding year, Cartier was able to learn from the Indians at Stadacona that there was another settlement of importance at Hochelaga, now Montreal. The navigator decided to use the remaining days of autumn in a visit to this settlement, although the Stadacona Indians strenuously objected, declaring that there were all manner of dangers and difficulties in the way. With his smallest vessel and about half of his men, Cartier, however, made his way up the river during the last fortnight in September.

Near the point where the largest of the St. Lawrence rapids bars the river gateway to the

west the Frenchman found Hochelaga nestling
between the mountain and the shore, in the midst
of "goodly and large fields full of corn such as the
country yieldeth." The Indian village, which
consisted of about fifty houses, was encircled by
three courses of palisades, one within the other.
The natives received their visitors with great
cordiality, and after a liberal distribution of trinkets the French learned from them some vague
snatches of information about the rivers and great
lakes which lay to the westward "where a man
might travel on the face of the waters for many
moons in the same direction." But as winter was
near Cartier found it necessary to hurry back to
Stadacona, where the remaining members of his
expedition had built a small fort or *habitation*
during his absence.

Everything was made ready for the long season
of cold and snow, but the winter came on with
unusual severity. The neighboring Indians grew
so hostile that the French hardly dared to venture
from their narrow quarters. Supplies ran low,
and to make matters worse the pestilence of scurvy
came upon the camp. In February almost the
entire company was stricken down and nearly one
quarter of them had died before the emaciated

survivors learned from the Indians that the bark of a white spruce tree boiled in water would afford a cure. The Frenchmen dosed themselves with the Indian remedy, using a whole tree in less than a week, but with such revivifying results that Cartier hailed the discovery as a genuine miracle.

When spring appeared, the remnant of the company, now restored to health and vigor, gladly began their preparations for a return to France. There was no ardor among them for a further exploration of this inhospitable land. As there were not enough men to handle all three of the ships, they abandoned one of them, whose timbers were uncovered from the mudbank in 1843, more than three centuries later. Before leaving Stadacona, however, Cartier decided to take Donnacona, the head of the village, and several other Indians as presents to the French King. It was natural enough that the master-pilot should wish to bring his sovereign some impressive souvenir from the new domains, yet this sort of treachery and ingratitude was unpardonable. Donnacona and all these captives but one little Indian maiden died in France, and his people did not readily forget the lesson of European duplicity. By July the expedition was back in the harbor of St.

Malo, and Cartier was promptly at work preparing for the King a journal of his experiences.

Cartier's account of his voyage which has come down to us contains many interesting details concerning the topography and life of the new land. The Malouin captain was a good navigator as seafaring went in his day, a good judge of distance at sea, and a keen observer of landmarks. But he was not a discriminating chronicler of those things which we would now wish to understand — for example, the relationship and status of the various Indian tribes with which he came into contact. All manner of Indian customs are superficially described, particularly those which presented to the French the aspect of novelty, but we are left altogether uncertain as to whether the Indians at Stadacona in Cartier's time were of Huron or Iroquois or Algonquin stock. The navigator did not describe with sufficient clearness, or with a due differentiation of the important from the trivial, those things which ethnologists would now like to know.

It must have been a disappointment not to be able to lay before the King any promise of great mineral wealth to be found in the new territory. While at Hochelaga Cartier had gleaned from the

Indians some vague allusions to sources of silver and copper in the far northwest, but that was all. He had not found a northern Eldorado, nor had his quest of a new route to the Indies been a whit more fruitful.   Cartier had set out with this as his main motive, but had succeeded only in finding that there was no such route by way of the St. Lawrence.   Though the King was much interested in his recital of courage and hardships, he was not fired with zeal for spending good money in the immediate equipping of another expedition to these inhospitable shores.

Not for five years after his return in 1536, therefore, did Cartier again set out for the St. Lawrence. This time his sponsor was the Sieur de Roberval, a nobleman of Picardy, who had acquired an ambition to colonize a portion of the new territory and who had obtained the royal endorsement of his scheme.   The royal patronage was not difficult to obtain when no funds were sought.   Accordingly in 1540 Roberval, who was duly appointed viceroy of the country, enlisted the assistance of Cartier in carrying out his plans. It was arranged that Cartier with three ships should sail from St. Malo in the spring of 1541, while Roberval's part of the expedition should set forth at the same time from Honfleur. But when May arrived Roberval was not ready and Cartier's ships set sail alone, with the understanding that Roberval would follow. Cartier in due course reached Newfoundland, where for six weeks he awaited his viceroy. At length, his patience exhausted, he determined to push on alone to Stadacona, where he arrived toward the end of August. The ships were unloaded and two of the vessels were sent back to France. The rest of the expedition prepared to winter at Cap Rouge, a short distance above the settlement. Once more Cartier made a short trip up the river to Hochelaga, but with no important incidents, and here the voyageur's journal comes to an end. He may have written more, but if so the pages have never been found. Henceforth the evidence as to his doings is less extensive and less reliable. On his return he and his band seem to have passed the winter at Cap Rouge more comfortably than the first hibernation six years before, for the French had now learned the winter hygiene of the northern regions. The Indians, however, grew steadily more hostile as the months went by, and Cartier, fearing that his small following might not fare well in the event of a general assault, deemed it wise to start for France when the river opened in the spring of 1542.

Cartier set sail from Quebec in May. Taking the southern route through the Gulf he entered, early in June, the harbor of what is now St. John's, Newfoundland. There, according to Hakluyt, the Breton navigator and his belated viceroy, Roberval, anchored their ships side by side. Roberval, who had been delayed nearly a year, was now on his way to join Cartier at Quebec and had put into the Newfoundland harbor to refit his ships after a stormy voyage. What passed between the two on the occasion of this meeting will never be known with certainty. We have only the brief statement that after a spirited interview Cartier was ordered by his chief to turn his ships about and accompany the expedition back to Quebec. Instead of doing so, he spread his sails during the night and slipped homeward to St. Malo, leaving the viceroy to his own resources. There are difficulties in the way of accepting this story, however, although it is not absolutely inconsistent with the official records, as some later historians seem to have assumed.[1]

[1] Justin Winsor, *Narrative and Critical History of America*, vol. iv., 58.

At any rate it was in no pleasant humor that Roberval now proceeded to the St. Lawrence and up to Cap Rouge, where he took possession of Cartier's post, sowed some grain and vegetables, and endeavored to prepare for the winter. His company of followers, having been recruited from the jails of France, proved as unruly as might have been expected. Discipline and order could only be maintained by the exercise of great severity. One of the malefactors was executed; others were given the lash in generous measure. The winter, moreover, proved to be terribly cold; supplies ran low, and the scurvy once again got beyond control. If anything, the conditions were even worse than those which Cartier had to endure seven years before. When spring arrived the survivors had no thought of anything but a prompt return to France. But Roberval bade most of them wait until with a small party he ventured a trip to the territory near what is now Three Rivers and the mouth of the St. Maurice. Apparently the whole party made its way safely back to France before the autumn, but as to how or when we have no record. There is some evidence that Cartier was sent out with a relief expedition in 1543, but in any case, both he and Roberval were in France during the spring of the next year, for they then appeared there in court to settle respective accounts of expenses incurred in the badly managed enterprise.

Of Cartier's later life little is known save that he lived at St. Malo until he died in 1557. With the exception of his journals, which cover only a part of his explorations, none of his writings or maps has come down to us. That he prepared maps is highly probable, for he was an explorer in the royal service. But diligent search on the part of antiquarians has not brought them to light. His portrait in the town hall at St. Malo shows us a man of firm and strong features with jaws tight-set, a high forehead, and penetrating eyes. Unhappily it is of relatively recent workmanship and as a likeness of the great Malouin its trustworthiness is at least questionable. Fearless and untiring, however, his own indisputable achievements amply prove him to have been. The tasks set before him were difficult to perform; he was often in tight places and he came through unscathed. As a navigator he possessed a skill that ranked with the best of his time. His was an intrepid sailor-soul. If his voyages resulted in no permanent establishment, that was not altogether

Cartier's fault. He was sent out on his first two voyages as an explorer, to find new trade routes, or stores of gold and silver or a rich land to exploit. On his third voyage, when a scheme of colonization was in hand, the failure of Roberval to do his part proved the undoing of the entire plan. There is no reason to believe that faint-heartedness or lack of courage had any place in Cartier's sturdy frame.

For sixty years following the ill-starred ventures of 1541–1542 no serious attempts were made to gain for France any real footing in the regions of the St. Lawrence. This is not altogether surprising, for there were troubles in plenty at home. Huguenots and Catholics had ranged themselves in civil strife; the wars of the Fronde were convulsing the land, and it was not until the very end of the sixteenth century that France settled down to peace within her own borders. Norman and Breton fishermen continued their yearly trips to the fishing-banks, but during the whole latter half of the sixteenth century no vessel, so far as we know, ever made its way beyond the Saguenay. Some schemes of colonization, without official support, were launched during this interval; but in all such cases the expeditions set forth to warmer lands, to Brazil and to Florida. In neither direction, however, did any marked success attend these praiseworthy examples of private initiative.

The great valley of the St. Lawrence during these six decades remained a land of mystery. The navigators of Europe still clung to the vision of a westward passage whose eastern portal must be hidden among the bays or estuaries of this silent land, but none was bold or persevering enough to seek it to the end. As for the great continent itself, Europe had not the slightest inkling of what it held in store for future generations of mankind.

CHAPTER III

In the closing years of the sixteenth century the spirit of French expansion, which had remained so strangely inactive for nearly three generations, once again began to manifest itself. The Sieur de La Roche, another Breton nobleman, the merchant traders, Pontgravé of St. Malo and Chauvin of Honfleur, came forward one after the other with plans for colonizing the unknown land. Unhappily these plans were not easily matured into stern realities. The ambitious project of La Roche came to grief on the barren sands of Sable Island. The adventurous merchants, for their part, obtained a monopoly of the trade and for a few years exploited the rich peltry regions of the St. Lawrence, but they made no serious attempts at actual settlement. Finally they lost the monopoly, which passed in 1603 to the Sieur de Chastes, a royal favorite and commandant at Dieppe.

It is at this point that Samuel Champlain first becomes associated with the pioneer history of New France.   Given the opportunity to sail with an expedition which De Chastes sent out in 1603, Champlain gladly accepted and from this time to the end of his days he never relaxed his whole-souled interest in the design to establish a French dominion in these western lands.   With his accession to the ranks of the voyageurs real progress in the field of colonization was for the first time assured.   Champlain encountered many setbacks during his initial years as a colonizer, but he persevered to the end.   When he had finished his work, France had obtained a footing in the St. Lawrence valley which was not shaken for nearly a hundred and fifty years.

Champlain was born in 1567 at the seaport of Brouage, on the Bay of Biscay, so that he was only thirty-six years of age when he set out on his first voyage to America.   His forbears belonged to the lesser gentry of Saintonge, and from them he inherited a roving strain.   Long before reaching middle manhood he had learned to face dangers, both as a soldier in the wars of the League and as a sailor to the Spanish Main.   With a love of adventure he combined rare powers of description,

so much so that the narrative of his early voyages
to this region had attracted the King's attention
and had won for him the title of royal geographer.
His ideas were bold and clear; he had an inflexible
will and great patience in battling with discourage-
ments.   Possessing these qualities, Champlain was
in every way fitted to become the founder of New
France.

The expedition of 1603 proceeded to the St.
Lawrence, where some of the party landed at the
mouth of the Saguenay to trade with the Indians.
The remainder, including Champlain, made their
way up the river to the Indian village at Hochelaga, which they now found in ruins, savage war-
fare having turned the place into a solitude.
Champlain busied himself with some study of the
country's resources and the customs of the abo-
rigines; but on the whole the prospects of the St.
Lawrence valley did not move the explorers to
enthusiasm.   Descending the great river again,
they rejoined their comrades at the Saguenay, and,
taking their cargoes of furs aboard, the whole
party sailed back to France in the autumn.   There
they found that De Chastes, the sponsor for their
enterprise, had died during their absence.

The death of De Chastes upset matters badly,

for with it the trade monopoly had lapsed. But
things were promptly set right again by a royal
act which granted the monopoly anew. This
time it went to the Sieur de Monts, a prominent
Huguenot nobleman, then governor of Pons, with
whom Champlain was on friendly terms. To
quiet the clamors of rival traders, however, it was
stipulated that Monts should organize a company
and should be bound to take into his enterprise
any who might wish to associate themselves with
him. The company, in return for its trading
monopoly, was to transport to the new domains
at least one hundred settlers each year.

Little difficulty was encountered in organizing
the company, since various merchants of St. Malo,
Honfleur, Rouen, and Rochelle were eager to take
shares. Preparations for sending out an expedition on a much larger scale than on any previous
occasion were soon under way, and in 1604 two
well-equipped vessels set forth. One of them went
to the old trading-post at the Saguenay; the other
went southward to the regions of Acadia. On
board the latter were De Monts himself, Champlain as chief geographer, and a young adventurer
from the ranks of the *noblesse*, Biencourt de Poutrincourt. The personnel of this expedition was

excellent: it contained no convicts; most of its members were artisans and sturdy yeomen. Rounding the tip of the Nova Scotian peninsula, these vessels came to anchor in the haven of Port Royal, now Annapolis. Not satisfied with the prospects there, however, they coasted around the Bay of Fundy, and finally reached the island in Passamaquoddy Bay which they named St. Croix. Here on June 25, 1604, the party decided to found their settlement. Work on the buildings was at once commenced, and soon the little colony was safely housed. In the autumn Poutrincourt was dispatched with one vessel and a crew back to France, while Champlain and the rest prepared to spend the winter in their new island home.

The choice of St. Croix as a location proved singularly unfortunate; the winter was long and severe, and the preparations that had been made were soon found to be inadequate. Once more there were sufferings such as Cartier and his men had undergone during the terrible winter of 1534–1535 at Quebec. There were no brooks or springs close at hand, and no fresh water except such as could be had by melting snow. The storehouse had no cellar, and in consequence the vegetables froze, so that the company was reduced to salted meat as the chief staple of diet. Scurvy ravaged the camp, and before the snows melted nearly two-fifths of the party had died. Not until June, moreover, did a vessel arrive from France with fresh stores and more colonists.

The experience of this first winter must have indeed "produced discontent," as Champlain rather mildly expressed it, but it did not impel De Monts to abandon his plans. St. Croix, however, was given up and, after a futile search for a better location on the New England coast, the colony moved across the bay to Port Royal, where the buildings were reconstructed. In the autumn De Monts went back to France, leaving Champlain, Pontgravé, and forty-three others to spend the winter of 1605–1606 in Acadia. During this hibernation the fates were far more kind. The season proved milder, the bitter lessons of the previous season had not gone unlearned, and scurvy did not make serious headway. But when June came and De Monts had not returned from France with fresh supplies, there was general discouragement; so much so that plans for the entire abandonment of the place were on the eve of being carried out when a large vessel rounded the point on its way into the Basin. Aboard were

Poutrincourt and Marc Lescarbot, together with more settlers and supplies. Lescarbot was a Parisian lawyer in search of adventure, a man who combined wit with wisdom, one of the pleasantest figures in the annals of American colonization. He was destined to gain a place in literary history as the interesting chronicler of this little colony's all-too-brief existence. These arrivals put new heart into the men, and they set to work sowing grain and vegetables, which grew in such abundance that the storehouses were filled to their capacity. The ensuing winter found the company with an ample store of everything. The season of ice and snow passed quickly, thanks largely to Champlain's successful endeavor to keep the colonists in good health and spirits by exercise, by variety in diet, and by divers gaieties under the auspices of his *Ordre de Bon Temps*, a spontaneous social organization created for the purpose of banishing cares and worries from the little settlement. It seemed as though the colony had been established to stay.

But with the spring of 1607 came news which quickly put an end to all this optimism. Rival merchants had been clamoring against the monopoly of the De Monts company. Despite the fact

that De Monts was a Huguenot and thus a shining
target for the shafts of bigotry, these protests had
for three years failed to move the King; but now
they had gained their point, and the monopoly
had come to an end.   This meant that there would
be no more ships with settlers or supplies.   As the
colony could not yet hope to exist on its own
resources, there was no alternative but to abandon
the site and return to France, and this the whole
party reluctantly proceeded to do.

On arrival in France the affairs of the company
were wound up, and De Monts found himself a
heavy loser.   He was not yet ready to quit the
game, however, and Champlain with the aid of
Pontgravé was able to convince him that a new
venture in the St. Lawrence region might yield
profits even without the protection of a monopoly.
Thus out of misfortune and failure arose the plans
which led to the founding of a permanent outpost
of empire at Quebec.

In the spring of 1608 Champlain and Pontgravé
once again set sail for the St. Lawrence.   The latter
delayed at the Saguenay to trade, while Champlain
pushed on to the site of the old Stadacona, where
at the foot of the cliff he laid the foundations of
the new Quebec, the first permanent settlement of

Europeans in the territory of New France. On the shore below the rocky steep several houses were built, and measures were taken to defend them in case of an Indian attack. Here Champlain's party spent the winter of 1608–1609.

With the experience gained at St. Croix and Port Royal it should have been possible to provide for all eventualities, yet difficulties in profusion were encountered during these winter months. First there was the unearthing of a conspiracy against Champlain. Those concerned in it were speedily punished, but the execution of the chief culprit gave to the new settlement a rather ominous beginning. Then came a season of zero weather, and the scurvy came with it. Champlain had heard of the remedy used by Cartier, but the tribes which had been at Stadacona in Cartier's time had now disappeared, and there was no one to point out the old-time remedy to the suffering garrison. So the scourge went on unchecked. The ravages of disease were so severe that, when a relief ship arrived in the early summer of 1609, all but eight of Champlain's party had succumbed.

Yet there was no thought of abandoning the settlement. The beginnings of Canada made astounding demands upon the fortitude and stamina of these dauntless voyageurs, but their store of courage was far from the point of exhaustion. They were ready not only to stay but to explore the territory inland, to traverse its rivers and lakes, to trudge through its forests afoot that they might find out for the King's information what resources the vast land held in its silent expanses. After due deliberation, therefore, it was decided that Champlain and four others should accompany a party of Huron and Algonquin Indians upon one of their forays into the country of the Iroquois, this being the only way in which the Frenchmen could be sure of their native guides. So the new allies set forth to the southeastward, passing up the Richelieu River and, traversing the lake which now bears his name, Champlain and his Indian friends came upon a war party of Iroquois near Ticonderoga and a forest fight ensued. The muskets of the French terrified the enemy tribesmen and they fled in disorder. In itself the incident was not of much account nor were its consequences so far-reaching as some historians would have us believe. It is true that Champlain's action put the French for the moment in the bad graces of the Iroquois; but the conclusion that this foray was chiefly responsible for the hostility of the great tribes during the whole ensuing century is altogether without proper historical foundation.

Revenge was a prominent Indian trait, as with many other peoples, but it could never of itself have determined the alignment of the Five Nations against the French during a period of nearly eight generations. From the situation of their territories, the Iroquois were the natural allies of the English and Dutch on the one hand, and the natural foes of the French on the other. Trade soon became the Alpha and the Omega of all tribal diplomacy, and the Iroquois were discerning enough to realize that their natural rôle was to serve as middlemen between the western Indians and the English. Their very livelihood, indeed, depended on their success in diverting the flow of the fur trade through the Iroquois territories, for by the middle of the seventeenth century there were no beavers left in their own country. Such a situation meant that they must promote trade between the western Indians and the English at Albany; but to promote trade with the English meant friendship with the English, and friendship with the English meant enmity with the French. Here is the true key to the long series of quarrels in which the Five Nations and New France engaged. Champlain's little escapade at Ticonderoga was a mere incident and the Iroquois would have soon forgotten it if their economic interests had required them to do so. "Trade and peace," said an Iroquois chief to the French on one occasion, "we take to be one thing." He was right; they have been one thing in all ages. As companions, trade and the flag have been inseparable in all lands. The expedition of 1609 had, however, some results besides the discomfiture of an Iroquois raiding party. It disclosed to the French a water-route which led almost to the upper reaches of the Hudson. The spot where Champlain put the Iroquois to flight is within thirty leagues of Albany. It was by this route that the French and English came so often into warring contact during the next one hundred and fifty years.

Explorations, the care of his little settlement at Quebec, trading operations, and two visits to France occupied Champlain's attention during the next few years. Down to this time no white man's foot had ever trodden the vast wilderness beyond the rapids above Hochelaga. Stories had filtered through concerning great waters far to the West and North, of hidden minerals there, and of fertile lands. Champlain was determined to see these things for himself and it was to that end that he made his two great trips to the interior, in 1613 and 1616, respectively.

The expedition of 1613 was not a journey of indefinite exploration; it had a very definite end in view. A few years previously Champlain had sent into the villages of the Algonquins on the upper Ottawa River a young Frenchman named Vignau, in order that by living for a time among these people he might learn their language and become useful as an interpreter. In 1612 Vignau came back with a marvelous story concerning a trip which he had made with his Algonquin friends to the Great North Sea where he had seen the wreck of an English vessel. This striking news inflamed Champlain's desire to find out whether this was not the route for which both Cartier and he himself had so eagerly searched — the western passage to Cathay and the Indies. There is evidence that the explorer from the first doubted the truth of Vignau's story, but in 1613 he decided to make sure and started up the Ottawa River, taking the young man with him to point the way.

After a fatiguing journey the party at length reached the Algonquin encampment on Allumette

Island in the upper Ottawa, where his doubts were fully confirmed. Vignau, the Algonquins assured Champlain, was an impostor; he had never been out of their sight, had never seen a Great North Sea; the English shipwreck was a figment of his imagination. "Overcome with wrath," writes Champlain, "I had him removed from my presence, being unable to bear the sight of him." The party went no further, but returned to Quebec. As for the impostor, the generosity of his leader in the end allowed him to go unpunished. Though the expedition had been in one sense a fool's errand and Champlain felt himself badly duped, yet it was not without its usefulness, for it gave him an opportunity to learn much concerning the methods of wilderness travel, the customs of the Indians and the extent to which they might be relied upon. The Algonquins and the Hurons had proved their friendship, but what they most desired, it now appeared, was that the French should give them substantial aid in another expedition against the Iroquois.

This was the basis upon which arrangements were made for Champlain's next journey to the interior, the longest and most daring enterprise in his whole career of exploration. In 1615 the

Brouage navigator with a small party once again ascended the Ottawa, crossed to Lake Nipissing and thence made his way down the French River to the Georgian Bay, or Lake of the Hurons as it was then called. Near the shores of the bay he found the villages of the Hurons with the Récollet Father Le Caron already at work among the tribesmen. Adding a large band of Indians to his party, the explorer now struck southeast and, by following the chain of small lakes and rivers which lie between Matchedash Bay and the Bay of Quinte, he eventually reached Lake Ontario. The territory pleased Champlain greatly, and he recorded his enthusiastic opinion of its fertility. Crossing the head of Lake Ontario in their canoes the party then headed for the country of the Iroquois south of Oneida Lake, where lay a palisaded village of the Onondagas. This they attacked, but after three hours' fighting were repulsed, Champlain being wounded in the knee by an Iroquois arrow.

The eleven Frenchmen with their horde of Indians then retreated cautiously; but the Onondagas made no serious attempt at pursuit, and in due course Champlain with his party recrossed Lake Ontario safely. The Frenchmen were now

eager to get back to Quebec by descending the St.
Lawrence, but their Indian allies would not hear
of this desertion. The whole expedition therefore
plodded on to the shores of the Georgian Bay,.
following a route somewhat north of the one by
which it had come. There the Frenchmen spent
a tedious winter. Champlain was anxious to
make use of the time by exploring the upper lakes,
but the task of settling some wretched feuds
among his Huron and Algonquin friends took
most of his time and energy. The winter gave
him opportunity, however, to learn a great deal
more about the daily life of the Indians, their
abodes, their customs, their agriculture, their
amusements, and their folklore. All this information went into his journals and would have been
of priceless value had not the Jesuits who came
later proved to be such untiring chroniclers of every
detail.

When spring came, Champlain left the Huron
country and by way of Lake Nipissing and the
Ottawa once more reached his own people at
Quebec. It took him forty days to make the
journey from the Georgian Bay to the present
site of Montreal.

Arriving at Quebec, where he was hailed as

one risen from the dead, Champlain found that
things in France had taken a new turn. They
had, in fact, taken many twists and turns during
the nine years since De Monts had financed the
first voyage to the St. Lawrence. In the first
place, De Monts had lost the last vestige of his
influence at court; as a Huguenot he could not
expect to have retained it under the stern regency
which followed the assassination of Henry IV
in 1610. Then a half-dozen makeshift arrangements came in the ensuing years. It was always
the same story faithfully repeated in its broad
outlines. Some friendly nobleman would obtain
from the King appointment as viceroy of New
France and at the same time a trading monopoly
for a term of years, always promising to send out
some settlers in return. The monopoly would
then be sublet, and Champlain would be recognized as a sort of viceroy's deputy. And all for a
colony in which the white population did not yet
number fifty souls!

Despite the small population, however, Champlain's task at Quebec was difficult and exacting.
His sponsors in France had no interest in the
permanent upbuilding of the colony; they sent out
very few settlers, and gave him little in the way

of funds. The traders who came to the St. Lawrence each summer were an unruly and boisterous crew who quarreled with the Indians and among themselves. At times, indeed, Champlain was sorely tempted to throw up the undertaking in disgust. But his patience held out until 1627, when the rise of Richelieu in France put the affairs of the colony upon a new and more active basis. For a quarter of a century, France had been letting golden opportunities slip by while the colonies and trade of her rivals were forging ahead. Spain and Portugal were secure in the South. England had gained firm footholds both in Virginia and on Massachusetts Bay. Even Holland had a strong commercial company in the field. This was a situation which no far-sighted Frenchman could endure. Hence Cardinal Richelieu, when he became chief minister of Louis XIII, undertook to see that France should have her share of New World spoils. "No realm is so well situated as France," he declared, "to be mistress of the seas or so rich in all things needful." The cardinal-minister combined fertility in ideas with such a genius for organization that his plans were quickly under way. Unhappily his talent for details, for the efficient handling of little things, was not nearly so great, and some of his arrangements went sadly awry in consequence.

At any rate Richelieu in 1627 prevailed upon the King to abolish the office of viceroy, to cancel all trading privileges, and to permit the organization of a great colonizing company, one that might hope to rival the English and Dutch commercial organizations. This was formed under the name of the Company of New France, or the Company of One Hundred Associates, as it was more commonly called from the fact that its membership was restricted to one hundred shareholders, each of whom contributed three thousand *livres*. The cardinal himself, the ministers of state, noblemen, and courtesans of Paris, as well as merchants of the port towns, all figured in the list of stockholders. The subscription lists contained an imposing array of names.

The powers of the new Company, moreover, were as imposing as its personnel. To it was granted a perpetual monopoly of the fur trade and of all other commerce with rights of suzerainty over all the territories of New France and Acadia. It was to govern these lands, levy taxes, establish courts, appoint officials, and even bestow titles of nobility. In return the Company undertook to convey to the colony not less than two hundred settlers per year, and to provide them with subsistence until they could become self-supporting. It was stipulated, however, that no Huguenots or other heretics should be among the immigrants.

The Hundred Associates entered upon this portentous task with promptness and enthusiasm. Early in 1628 a fleet of eighteen vessels freighted with equipment, settlers, and supplies set sail from Dieppe for the St. Lawrence to begin operations. But the time of its arrival was highly inopportune, for France was now at war with England, and it happened that a fleet of English privateers was already seeking prey in the Lower St. Lawrence. These privateers, commanded by Kirke, intercepted the Company's heavily-laden caravels, overpowered them, and carried their prizes off to England. Thus the Company of the One Hundred Associates lost a large part of its capital, and its shareholders received a generous dividend of disappointment in the very first year of its operations.

A more serious blow, however, was yet to come. Flushed with his success in 1628, Kirke came back to the St. Lawrence during the next summer and proceeded to Quebec, where he summoned Champlain and his little settlement to surrender. As the place was on the verge of famine owing to the capture of the supply ships in the previous year, there was no alternative but to comply, and the colony passed for the first time into English hands. Champlain was allowed to sail for England, where he sought the services of the French ambassador and earnestly advised that the King be urged to insist on the restoration of Canada whenever the time for peace should come. Negotiations for peace soon began, but they dragged on tediously until 1632, when the Treaty of St. Germain-en-Laye gave back New France to its former owners.

With this turn in affairs the Company was able to resume its operations. Champlain, as its representative, once more reached Quebec, where he received a genuine welcome from the few Frenchmen who had remained through the years of Babylonian captivity, and from the bands of neighboring Indians. With his hands again set to the arduous tasks, Champlain was able to make substantial progress during the next two years. For a time the Company gave him funds and equipment besides sending him some excellent colonists. Lands were cleared in the neighborhood of the settlement; buildings were improved and enlarged; trade with the Indians was put upon a better basis. A post was established at Three Rivers, and plans were made for a further extension of French influence to the westward. It was in the midst of these achievements and hopes that Champlain was stricken by paralysis and died on Christmas Day, 1635.

Champlain's portrait, attributed to Moncornet, shows us a sturdy, broad-shouldered frame, with features in keeping. Unhappily we have no assurance that it is a faithful likeness. No one, however, can deny that the mariner of Brouage, with his extraordinary perseverance and energy, was admirably fitted to be the pathfinder to a new realm. Not often does one encounter in the annals of any nation a man of greater tenacity and patience. Chagrin and disappointment he had to meet on many occasions, but he was never baffled nor moved to concede defeat. His perseverance, however, was not greater than his modesty, for never in his writings did he magnify his difficulties nor exalt his own powers of overcoming them, as was too much the fashion of his day. As a writer, his style was plain and direct, with no attempt at embellishment and no indication that strong emotions ever had much influence upon his pen.   He was essentially a man of action, and his narrative is in the main a simple record of such a man's achievements.   His character was above reproach; no one ever impugned his honesty or his sincere devotion to the best interests of his superiors.   To his Church he was loyal in the last degree; and it was under his auspices that the first of the Jesuit missionaries came to begin the enduring work which the Order was destined to accomplish in New France.

On the death of Champlain the Company appointed the Sieur de Montmagny to be governor of the colony.   He was an ardent sympathizer with the aims of the Jesuits, and life at Quebec soon became almost monastic in its austerity. The Jesuits sent home each year their *Rélations*, and, as these were widely read, they created great interest in the spiritual affairs of the colony.   The call for zealots to carry the cross westward into the wilderness met ready response, and it was amid a glow of religious fervor that the settlement at Montreal was brought into being.   A company was formed in France, funds were obtained, and a band of forty-four colonists was recruited for the crusade into the wilderness.   The Sieur de Maisonneuve, a gallant soldier and a loyal devotee of the Church, was the active leader of the enterprise, with Jeanne Mance, an ardent young religionist of high motives and fine character, as his principal coadjutor. Fortune dealt kindly with the project, and Montreal began its history in 1642.

A few years later Montmagny gave up his post and returned to France. With the limited resources at his disposal, he had served the colony well, and had left it stronger and more prosperous than when he came. His successor was M. D'Ailleboust, who had been for some time in the country, and who was consequently no stranger to its needs. On his appointment a council was created, to consist of the governor of the colony, the bishop or the superior of the Jesuits, and the governor of Montreal. Henceforth this body was to be responsible for the making of all general regulations. It is commonly called the Old Council to distinguish it from the Sovereign Council by which it was supplanted in 1663.

The opening years of the new administration were marked by one of the greatest of forest tragedies, the destruction of the Hurons. In 1648 a party of Iroquois warriors made their way across Lake Ontario and overland to the Huron country, where they destroyed one large

village. Emboldened by this success, a much
larger body of the tribesmen returned in the year
following and completed their bloody work. A
dozen or more Huron settlements were attacked
and laid waste with wanton slaughter. Two
Jesuit priests, Lalemant and Brébeuf, who were
laboring among the Hurons, were taken and
burned at the stake after suffering atrocious
tortures. The remnants of the tribe were scattered: a few found shelter on the islands of the
Georgian Bay, while others took refuge with
the French and were given a tract of land at
Sillery, near Quebec. To the French colony the
extirpation of the Hurons came as a severe blow.
It weakened their prestige in the west, it cut off
a lucrative source of fur supply, and it involved
the loss of faithful allies.

More ominous still, the Iroquois by the success
of their forays into the Huron country endangered
the French settlement at Montreal. Glorying
in their prowess, these warriors now boasted
that they would leave the Frenchmen no peace
but in their graves. And they proceeded to make
good their threatenings. Bands of confederates
spread themselves about the region near Montreal,
pouncing lynx-like from the forest upon any who

ventured outside the immediate boundaries of the settlement. For a time the people were in despair, but the colony soon gained a breathing space, not by its own efforts, but from a diversion of Iroquois enmity to other quarters.

About 1652 the confederated tribes undertook their famous expedition against the Eries, whose country lay along the south shore of the lake which bears their name, and this enterprise for the time absorbed the bulk of the Iroquois energy. The next governor of New France, De Lauzon, regarded the moment as opportune for peace negotiations, on the hypothesis that the idea of waging only one war at a time might appeal to the Five Nations as sound policy. A mission was accordingly sent to the Iroquois, headed by the Jesuit missionary Le Moyne, and for a time it seemed as if arrangements for a lasting peace might be made. But there was no sincerity in the Iroquois professions. Their real interest lay in peaceful relations with the Dutch and the English; the French were their logical enemies; and when the Iroquois had finished with the Eries their insolence quickly showed itself once more.

The next few years therefore found the colony

again in desperate straits. In its entire population there were not more than five hundred men capable of taking the field, nor were there firearms for all of these. The Iroquois confederacy could muster at least three times that number; they were now obtaining firearms in plenty from the Dutch at Albany; and they could concentrate their whole assault upon the French settlement at Montreal. Had the Iroquois known the barest elements of siege operations, the colony must have come to a speedy and disastrous end. As the outcome proved, however, they were unwise enough to divide their strength and to dissipate their energies in isolated raids, so that Montreal came safely through the gloomy years of 1658 and 1659.

In the latter of these years there arrived from France a man who was destined to play a large part in its affairs during the next few decades, François-Xavier de Laval, who now came to take charge of ecclesiastical affairs in New France with the powers of a vicar apostolic. Laval's arrival did not mark the beginning of friction between the Church and the civil officials in the colony; there were such dissensions already. But the doughty churchman's claims and the governor's policy of resisting them soon brought things to an open breach, particularly upon the question of permitting the sale of liquor to the Indians. In 1662 the quarrel became bitter. Laval hastened home to France where he placed before the authorities the list of ecclesiastical grievances. The governor, a bluff old soldier, was thereupon summoned to Paris to present his side of the whole affair. In the end a decision was reached to reorganize the whole system of civil and commercial administration in the colony. Thus, as we shall soon see, the power passed away altogether from the Company of One Hundred Associates.

CHAPTER IV

Louis XIV, the greatest of the Bourbon monarchs, had now taken into his own hands the reins of power. Nominally he had been king of France since 1642, when he was only five years old, but it was not until 1658 that the control of affairs by the regency came to an end. Moreover, Colbert was now chief minister of state, so that colonial matters were assured of a searching and enlightened inquiry. Richelieu's interest in the progress of New France had not endured for many years after the founding of his great Company. It is true that during the next fifteen years he remained chief minister, but the great effort to crush the remaining strongholds of feudalism and to centralize all political power in the monarchy left him no time for the care of a distant colony. Colbert, on the other hand, had well-defined and far-reaching plans for the development of French industrial interests at home and of French commercial interests abroad.

As for the colony, it made meager progress under Company control: few settlers were sent out; and they were not provided with proper means of defense against Indian depredations. Under the circumstances it did not take Colbert long to see how remiss the Company of One Hundred Associates had been, nor to reach a decision that the colony should be at once withdrawn from its control. He accordingly persuaded the monarch to demand the surrender of the Company's charter and to reprimand the Associates for the shameless way in which they had neglected the trust committed to their care. "Instead of finding," declared the King in the edict of revocation, "that this country is populated as it ought to be after so long an occupation thereof by our subjects, we have learned with regret not only that the number of its inhabitants is very limited, but that even these are daily exposed to the danger of being wiped out by the Iroquois."

In truth, the company had little to show for its thirty years of exploitation. The entire population of New France in 1663 numbered less than twenty-five hundred people, a considerable proportion of whom were traders, officials, and priests. The area of cleared land was astonishingly small, and agriculture had made no progress worthy of the name. There were no industries of any kind, and almost nothing but furs went home in the ships to France. The colony depended upon its mother country even for its annual food supply, and when the ships from France failed to come the colonists were reduced to severe privations. A dispirited and nearly defenseless land, without solid foundations of agriculture or industry, with an accumulation of Indian enmity and an empty treasury—this was the legacy which the Company now turned over to the Crown in return for the viceroyal privileges given to it in good faith more than three decades before.

When the King revoked the Company's charter, he decided upon Colbert's advice to make New France a royal domain and to provide it with a scheme of administration modeled broadly upon that of a province at home. To this end a royal edict, perhaps the most important of all the many decrees affecting French colonial interests in the seventeenth century, was issued in April, 1663. While the provisions of this edict bear the stamp of Colbert's handiwork, it is not unlikely that the suggestions of Bishop Laval, as given to the minister during his visit of the preceding year, were accorded some recognition. At any rate, after reciting the circumstances under which the King had been prompted to take New France into his own hands, the edict of 1663 proceeded to authorize the creation of a Sovereign Council as the chief governing body of the colony. This, with a larger membership and with greatly increased powers, was to replace the old council which the Company had established to administer affairs some years previously.

During the next hundred years this Sovereign Council became and remained the paramount civil authority in French America. At the outset it consisted of seven members, the governor and the bishop *ex officio*, with five residents of the colony selected jointly by these two. Beginning with the arrival of Talon as first intendant of the colony in 1665, the occupant of this post was also given a seat in the Council. Before long, however, it became apparent that the provision relating to the appointment of non-official members was unworkable. The governor and the bishop could not agree in their selections; each wanted his own

partisans appointed. The result was a deadlock
in which seats at the council-board remained
vacant. In the end Louis Quatorze solved this
problem, as he solved many others, by taking the
power directly into his own hands. After 1674
all appointments to the Council were made by
the King himself. In that same year the number
of non-official members was raised to seven, and in
1703 it was further increased to twelve.[1] At the
height of its power, then, the Sovereign Council
of New France consisted of the governor, the
intendant, the bishop, and twelve lay councilors,
together with an attorney-general and a clerk.
These two last-named officials sat with the Council
but were not regular members of it.

In the matter of powers the Council was given
by the edict of 1663 jurisdiction over all civil and
criminal matters under the laws and ordinances of
the kingdom, its procedure in dealing with such
matters to be modeled on that of the Parliament
of Paris. It was to receive and to register the
royal decrees, thus giving them validity in New
France, and it was also to be the supreme tribunal
of the colony with authority to establish local
courts subordinate to itself. There was no

[1] Its official title was in 1678 changed to Superior Council.

division of powers in the new frame of government. Legislative, executive, and judicial powers were thrown together in true Bourbon fashion. Apparently it was Colbert's plan to make of the governor a distinguished figurehead, with large military powers but without paramount influence in civil affairs. The bishop was to have no civil jurisdiction, and the intendant was to be the director of details. The Council, according to the edict of 1663, was to be the real pivot of power in New France.

Through the long years of storm and stress which make up the greater part of the history of the colony, the Sovereign Council rendered diligent and faithful service. There were times when passions waxed warm, when bitter words were exchanged, and when the urgent interests of the colony were sacrificed to the settlement of personal jealousies. Many dramatic scenes were enacted around the long table at which the councilors sat at their weekly sessions, for every Monday through the greater portion of the year the Council convened at seven o'clock in the morning and usually sat until noon or later. But these were only meteoric flashes. Historians have given them undue prominence because such episodes make racy reading. By far the greater portion of the council's meetings were devoted to the serious and patient consideration of routine business. Matters of infinite variety came to it for determination, including the regulation of industry and trade, the currency, the fixing of prices, the interpretation of the rules relating to land tenure, fire prevention, poor relief, regulation of the liquor traffic, the encouragement of agriculture—and these are only a few of the topics taken at random from its calendar. In addition there were thousands of disputes brought to it for settlement either directly or on appeal from the lower courts. The minutes of its deliberations during the ninety-seven years from September 18, 1663, to April 8, 1760, fill no fewer than fifty-six ponderous manuscript volumes.

Though, in the edict establishing the Sovereign Council, no mention was made of an intendant, the decision to send such an official to New France came very shortly thereafter. In 1665 Jean Talon arrived at Quebec bearing a royal commission which gave him wide powers, infringing to some extent on the authority vested in the Sovereign Council two years previously. The phraseology was similar to that used in the commissions of the

provincial intendants in France, and so broad was
the wording, indeed, that one might well ask
what other powers could be left for exercise by
any one else.   No wonder that the seventeenth-
century apostle of frenzied finance, John Law,
should have laconically described France as a land
"ruled by a king and his thirty intendants, upon
whose will alone its welfare and its wants depend."
Along with his commission Talon brought to the
colony a letter of instructions from the minister
which gave more detailed directions as to what
things he was to have in view and what he was to
avoid.

In France the office of intendant had long been in
existence.   Its creation in the first instance has
commonly been attributed to Richelieu, but it
really antedated the coming of the great cardinal.   The intendancy was not a spontaneous
creation, but a very old and, in its origin, a humble
post which grew in importance with the centralization of power in the King's hands, and which
kept step in its development with the gradual
extinction of local self-government in the royal
domains.   The provincial intendant in pre-revo-
lutionary France was master of administration,
finance, and justice within his own jurisdiction; he

was bound by no rigid statutes; he owed obedience
to no local authorities; he was appointed by the
King and was responsible to his sovereign alone.

From first to last there were a dozen intendants
of New France.   Talon, whose ambition and
energy did much to set the colony in the saddle, was
the first.   François Bigot, the arch-plunderer of
his monarch's funds, who did so much to bring
the land to its downfall, was the last.   Between
them came a line of sensible, earnest, hard-working
officials who served their King far better than they
served themselves, who gave the best years of their
lives to the task of making New France a bright
jewel in the Bourbon crown.   The colonial intendant was the royal man-of-all-work.   The King
spoke and the intendant forthwith transformed his
words into action.   As the King's great interest
in New France, coupled with his scant knowledge
of its conditions, moved him to speak often, and
usually in broad generalities, the intendant's
activity was prodigious and his discretion wide.
Ordinances and decrees flew from his pen like
sparks from a blacksmith's forge.   The duty
devolved upon him as the overseas apostle of
Gallic paternalism to "order everything as seemed
just and proper," even when this brought his hand

into the very homes of the people, into their daily work or worship or amusements. Nothing that needed setting aright was too inconsequential to have an ordinance devoted to it. As general regulator of work and play, of manners and morals, of things present and things to come, the intendant was the busiest man in the colony.

In addition to the governor, the council, and the intendant, there were many other officials on the civil list. Both the governor and the intendant had their deputies at Montreal and at Three Rivers. There were judges and bailiffs and seneschals and local officers by the score, not to speak of those who held sinecures or received royal pensions. There were garrisons to be maintained at all the frontier posts and church officials to be supported by large sums. No marvel it was that New France could never pay its own way. Every year there was a deficit which the King had to liquidate by payments from the royal exchequer.

The administration of the colony, moreover, fell far short of even reasonable efficiency. There were far too many officials for the relatively small amount of work to be done, and their respective fields of authority were inadequately defined. Too often the work of these officials lacked even the semblance of harmony, nor did the royal authorities always view this deficiency with regret. A fair amount of working at cross-purposes, provided it did not bring affairs to a complete standstill, was regarded as a necessary system of checks and balances in a colony which lay three thousand miles away. It prevented any chance of a general conspiracy against the home authorities or any wholesale wrong-doing through collusion. It served to make every official a ready tale-bearer in all matters concerning the motives and acts of his colleagues, so that the King might with reasonable certainty count upon hearing all the sides to every story. That, in fact, was wholly in consonance with Latin traditions of government, and it was characteristically the French way of doing things in the seventeenth and eighteenth centuries.

Louis XIV took a great personal interest in New France even to the neglect at times of things which his courtiers deemed to be far more important. The governor and the intendant plied him with their requests, with their grievances, and too often with their prosy tales of petty squabbling. With every ship they sent to Versailles their *mémoires*, often of intolerable length;

and the patient monarch read them all.   Marginal notes, made with his own hand, are still upon many of them, and the student who plods his way through the musty bundles of official correspondence in the *Archives Nationales* will find in these marginal comments enough to convince him that, whatever the failings of Louis XIV may have been, indolence was not of them.   Then with the next ships the King sent back his budget of orders, counsel, reprimand, and praise.   If the colony failed to thrive, it was not because the royal interest in it proved insincere or deficient.

The progress of New France, as reported in these dispatches from Quebec, with their figures of slow growth in population, of poor crops, and of failing trade, of Indian troubles and dangers from the English, of privations at times and of deficits always, must often have dampened the royal hopes.   The requests for subsidies from the royal purse were especially relentless.   Every second dispatch contained pleas for money or for things which were bound to cost money if the King provided them: money to enable some one to clear his lands, or to start an industry, or to take a trip of exploration to the wilds; money to provide more priests, to build churches, or to repair fortifications; money to pension officials — the call for money was incessant year after year. In the face of these multifarious demands upon his exchequer, Louis XIV was amazingly generous, but the more he gave, the more the colony asked from him. Until the end of his days, he never failed in response if the object seemed worthy of his support. It was not until the Grand Monarch was gathered to his fathers that the officials of New France began to ply their requests in vain.

So much for the frame of government in the colony during the age of Louis XIV. Now as to the happenings during the decade following 1663. The new administration made a promising start under the headship of De Mézy, a fellow townsman and friend of Bishop Laval, who arrived in the autumn of 1663 to take up his duties as governor. In a few days he and the bishop had amicably chosen the five residents of the colony who were to serve as councilors, and the council began its sessions. But troubles soon loomed into view, brought on in part by Laval's desire to settle up some old scores now that he had the power as a member of the Sovereign Council and was the dominating influence in its deliberations. Under the bishop's inspiration the Council ordered the seizure of some papers belonging to Péronne Dumesnil, a former agent of the now defunct Company of One Hundred Associates. Dumesnil retorted by filing a *dossier* of charges against some of the councilors; and the colonists at once ranged themselves into two opposing factions — those who believed the charges and those who did not. The bishop had become the stormy petrel of colonial politics, and nature had in truth well fitted him for just such a rôle.

Soon, moreover, the relations between Mézy and Laval themselves became less cordial. For a year the governor had proved ready to give way graciously on every point; but there was a limit to his amenability, and now his proud spirit began to chafe under the dictation of his ecclesiastical colleague. At length he ventured to show a mind of his own; and then the breach between him and Laval widened quickly. Three of the councillors having joined the bishop against him, Mézy undertook a *coup d'état*, dismissed these councilors from their posts, and called a mass-meeting of the people to choose their successors. On the governor's part this was a serious tactical error. He could hardly expect that a monarch who was doing his best to crush out the last vestige of representative government in France would welcome its establishment and encouragement by one of his own officials in the New World. But Mézy did not live to obey the recall which speedily came from the King as the outcome of this indiscretion. In the spring of 1665 he was taken ill and died at Quebec. "He went to rest among the paupers," says Parkman, "and the priests, serenely triumphant, sang requiems over his grave."

But discord within its borders was not the colony's only trouble during these years. The scourge of the Iroquois was again upon the land. During the years 1663 and 1664 bands of Mohawks and Oneidas raided the regions of the Richelieu and penetrated to the settlement at Three Rivers. These *petites guerres* were making things intolerable for the colonists, and the King was urged to send out a force of troops large enough to crush the bothersome Indians once for all. This plea met with a ready response, and in June, 1665, Prouville de Tracy with two hundred officers and men of the Régiment de Carignan-Salières disembarked at Quebec. The remaining companies of the regiment, making a force almost a thousand strong, arrived a little later. The people were now sure that deliverance was at hand, and the whole colony was in a frenzy of joy.

Following the arrival of the troops came Courcelle, the new governor, and Jean Talon, who was to take the post of intendant. These were gala days in New France; the whole colony had caught the spirit of the new imperialism. The banners and the trumpets, the scarlet cloaks and the perukes, the glittering profusion of gold lace and feathers, the clanking of swords and muskets, transformed Quebec in a season from a wilderness village to a Versailles in miniature. But there was little time for dress parades and affairs of ceremony. Tracy had come to give the Iroquois their *coup de grâce*, and the work must be done quickly. The King could not afford to have a thousand soldiers of the grand army eating their heads off through the long months of a Canadian winter.

The work of getting the expedition ready, therefore, was pushed rapidly ahead. Snowshoes were provided for the regiment, provisions and supplies were gathered, and in January, 1666, the expedition started up the frozen Richelieu, traversed Lake Champlain, and moved across to the headwaters of the Hudson. It was a spectacle new to the northern wilderness of America, this glittering and picturesque cavalcade of regulars flanked by troops of militiamen and bands of fur-clothed Indians

moving on its errand of destruction along the
frozen rivers. But the French regular troops
were not habituated to long marches on snowshoes
in the dead of winter; and they made progress so
slowly that the Dutch settlers of the region had
time to warn the Mohawks of the approach of the
expedition. This upset all French plans, since the
leaders had hoped to fall upon the Mohawk
villages and to destroy them before the tribesmen
could either make preparations for defense or
withdraw southward. Foiled in this plan, and
afraid that an early thaw might make their route
of return impossible, the French gave up their
project and started home again. They had not
managed to reach, much less to destroy, the
villages of their enemies.

But the undertaking was not an absolute failure.
The Mohawks were astute enough to see that only
the inexperience of the French had stood between
them and destruction. Here was an enemy which
had proved able to come through the dead of
winter right into the regions which had hitherto
been regarded as inaccessible from the north. The
French might be depended to come again and, by
reason of greater experience, to make a better job
of their coming. The Iroqucis reasoning was quite

correct, as the sequel soon disclosed. In September of the same year the French had once again equipped their expedition, more effectively this time. Traveling overland along nearly the same route, it reached the country of the Mohawks without a mishap. The Indians saved themselves by a rapid flight to the forests, but their palisaded strongholds were demolished, their houses set afire, their *cachés* of corn dug out and destroyed. The Mohawks were left to face the oncoming winter with nothing but the woods to shelter them. Having finished their task of punishment, Tracy and his regiment made their way leisurely back to Quebec.

The Mohawks were now quite ready to make terms, and in 1667 they sent a delegation to Quebec to proffer peace. Two raids into their territories in successive years had taught them that they could not safely leave their homes to make war against the tribes of the west so long as the French were their enemies. And the desire to dominate the region of the lakes was a first principle of Iroquois policy at this time. An armistice was accordingly concluded, which lasted without serious interruption for more than a decade. One of the provisions of the peace was that Jesuit missions should be established in the Iroquois territory, this being the usual way in which the French assured themselves of diplomatic intercourse with the tribes.

With its trade routes once more securely open, New France now began a period of marked prosperity. Tracy and his staff went back to France, but most of his soldiers remained and became settlers. Wives for these soldiers were sent out under royal auspices, and liberal grants of money were provided to get the new households established. Since 1664, the trade of the colony had been once more in the hands of a commercial organization, the Company of the West Indies, whose financial success was, for the time being, assured by the revival of the fur traffic. Industries were beginning to spring into being, the population was increasing rapidly, and the King was showing a lively interest in all the colony's affairs. It was therefore a prosperous and promising colony to which Governor Frontenac came in 1672.

CHAPTER V

THE ten years following 1663 form a decade of extraordinary progress in the history of New France. The population of the colony had trebled, and now numbered approximately seven thousand; the red peril, thanks to Tracy's energetic work, had been lessened; while the fur trade had grown to large and lucrative proportions. With this increase in population and prosperity, there came a renaissance of enthusiasm for voyages of exploration and for the widening of the colony's frontiers. Glowing reports went home to the King concerning the latent possibilities of the New World. What the colony now needed was a strong and vigorous governor who would not only keep a firm hold upon what had been already achieved, but one who would also push on to greater and more glorious things.

It was in keeping with this spirit of faith and

hope that the King sent to Quebec, in 1672, Louis
de Buade, Count Frontenac, naming him governor
of all the French domains in North America.
Fifty-two years of age when he came to Canada,
Frontenac had been a soldier from his youth; he
had fought through hard campaigns in Italy, in
the Low Countries, and with the Venetians in their
defense of Candia against the Turks.   In fact, he
had but shortly returned from this last service
when he was chosen to succeed Courcelle as the
royal representative in New France.

To Frontenac's friends the appointment seemed
more like a banishment than a promotion.   But
there were several reasons why the governor
should have accepted gladly.   He had inherited
only a modest fortune, and most of this had been
spent, for thrift was not one of Frontenac's virtues.
His domestic life had not been happy, and there
were no strong personal ties binding him to life
in France.[1]   Moreover, the post of governor in
the colony was not to be judged by what it
had been in the days of D'Avaugour or De
Mézy.   The reports sent home by Talon had

[1] Saint-Simon, in his *Mémoires*, prints the current Parisian gossip
that Frontenac was sent to New France to shield him from the imperious temper of his wife and to afford him a means of livelihood.

stirred the national ambitions. "I am no courtier," this intendant had written, "and it is not to please the King or without reason that I say this portion of the French monarchy is going to become something great. What I now see enables me to make such a prediction." And indeed the figures of growth in population, of acreage cleared, and of industries rising into existence seemed to justify the intendant's optimism. Both the King and his ministers were building high hopes on Canada, as their choice of Frontenac proves, and in their selection of a man to carry out their plans they showed, on the whole, good judgment. Frontenac proved to be the ablest and most commanding of all the officials who served the Bourbon monarchy in the New World. In the long line of governors he approached most nearly to what a Viceroy ought to be.

It is true that in New France there were conditions which no amount of experience in the Old World could train a man to handle. Nor was Frontenac particularly fitted by training or temperament for all of the duties which his new post involved. In some things he was wellendowed; he had great physical endurance, a strong will, with no end of courage, and industry

to spare. These were qualities of the highest
value in a land encircled by enemies and forced
to depend for existence upon the strength of its
own people. But more serviceable still was his
ability in adapting himself to a new environment.
Men past fifty do not often show this quality in
marked degree, but Frontenac fitted himself to
the novelty of colonial life exceedingly well. In
his relations with the Indians he showed amazing
skill. No other colonial governor, English, French,
or Dutch, ever commanded so readily the respect
and admiration of the red man. But in his dealings with the intendant and the bishop, with the
clergy, and with all those among the French of
New France who showed any disposition to dis-
agree with him, Frontenac displayed an uncon-
trollable temper, an arrogance of spirit, and a
degree of personal vanity which would not have
made for cordial relations in any field of human
effort. He had formed his own opinions and was
quite ready to ride rough-shod over those of other
men. It was this impetuosity that served to make
the official circles of the colony, during many
months of his term, a "little hell of discord."

But when the new viceroy arrived at Quebec
he was in high fettle; he was pleased with the

situation of the town and flattered by the enthusiastic greeting which he received from its people. His first step was to familiarize himself with the existing machinery of colonial government, which he found to be far from his liking. He proceeded, accordingly, in his own imperious way, to make some startling changes. For one thing, he decided to summon a representative assembly made up of the clergy, the seigneurs, and the common folk of New France. This body he brought together for his inauguration in October, 1672. No such assembly had ever been convened before, and nothing like it was ever allowed to assemble again. Before another year had passed, the minister sent Frontenac a polite reprimand with the intimation that the King could not permit in the colony an institution he was doing his best, and with entire success, to crush out at home. The same fate awaited the governor's other project, the establishment of a municipal government in the town of Quebec. Within a few months of his arrival, Frontenac had allowed the people of the town to elect a syndic and two aldermen, but the minister vetoed this action with the admonition that "you should very rarely, or, to speak more correctly, never, give a corporate voice to the inhabitants, for . . . it is well that each should speak for himself, and no one for all." In the reorganization of colonial administration, therefore, the governor found himself promptly called to a halt. He therefore turned to another field where he was much more successful in having his own way.

From the day of his arrival at Quebec the governor saw the pressing need of extending French influence and control into the regions bordering upon the Great Lakes. To dissipate the colony's efforts in westward expansion, however, was exactly what he had been instructed not to do. The King and his ministers were sure that it would be far wiser to devote all available energies and funds to developing the settled portions of the land. They desired the governor to carry on the policy of encouraging agriculture which Talon had begun, thus solidifying the colony and making its borders less difficult to defend. Frontenac's instructions on this point could hardly have been more explicit. "His Majesty considers it more consistent with the good of his service," wrote Colbert, "that you apply yourself to clearing and settling the most fertile places that are nearest the seacoast and the communication with France than to think afar of explorations in the interior of the country, so distant that they can never be inhabited by Frenchmen." This was discouraging counsel, showing neither breadth of vision nor familiarity with the urgent needs of the colony. Frontenac courageously set these instructions aside, and in doing so he was wise. Had he held to the letter of his instructions, New France would never have been more than a strip of territory fringing the Lower St. Lawrence. More than any other Frenchman he helped to plan the great empire of the West.

Notwithstanding the narrow views of his superiors at Versailles, Frontenac was convinced that the colony could best secure its own defense by controlling the chief line of water communications between the Iroquois country and Montreal. To this end he prepared to build a fort at Cataraqui where the St. Lawrence debouches from Lake Ontario. He was not, however, the first to recognize the strategic value of this point. Talon had marked it as a place of importance some years before, and the English authorities at Albany had been urged by the Iroquois chiefs to forestall any attempt that the French might make by being first on the ground. But the English procrastinated, and in the summer of 1673 the governor, with an imposing array of troops and militia, made his way to Cataraqui, having first summoned the Iroquois to meet him there in solemn council. In rather high dudgeon they came, ready to make trouble if the chance arose; but Frontenac's display of armed strength, his free-handed bestowal of presents, his tactful handling of the chiefs, and his effective oratory at the conclave soon assured him the upper hand. The fort was built, and the Iroquois, while they continued to regard it as an invasion of their territories, were forced to accept the new situation with reluctant grace.

This stroke at Cataraqui inflamed the governor's interest in western affairs. During his conferences with the Indians he had heard much about the great waters to the West and the rich beaver lands which lay beyond. He was ready, therefore, to encourage in every way the plans of those who wished to undertake journeys of exploration and trade into these regions, even although he was well aware that such enterprises would win little commendation from his superiors at the royal court. Voyageurs ready to undertake these tasks there were in plenty, and all of them found in the

Iron Governor a stalwart friend. Foremost among these pioneers of the Far Country was Robert Cavelier de La Salle, whom Frontenac had placed for a time in command of the fort at Cataraqui and who, in 1678, was commissioned by the governor to forge another link in the chain by the erection of a fort at Niagara. There he also built a small vessel, the first to ply the waters of the upper lakes, and in this La Salle and his lieutenants made their way to Michilimackinac. How he later journeyed to the Mississippi and down that stream to its mouth is a story to be told later on in these pages. It was and will remain a classic in the annals of exploration. And without Frontenac's vigorous support it could never have been accomplished. La Salle, when he performed his great feat of daring and endurance, was still a young man under forty, but his courage, firmness, and determination were not surpassed by any of his race. He had qualities that justified the confidence which the governor reposed in him.

But while La Salle was the most conspicuous among the pathfinders of this era, he was not the only one. Tonty, Du Lhut, La Forêt, La Mothe-Cadillac, and others were all in Frontenac's favor, and all had his vigorous support in their work.

Intrepid woodsmen, they covered every portion of the western wilderness, building forts and posts of trade, winning the friendship of the Indians, planting the arms of France in new soil and carrying the *Vexilla Regis* into parts unknown before. If Frontenac could have had his way, if the King had provided him with the funds, he would have run an iron chain of fortified posts all along the great water routes from Cataraqui to the Mississippi — and he had lieutenants who were able to carry out such an undertaking. But there were great obstacles in the way,—the lukewarmness of the home government, the bitter opposition of the Jesuits, and the intrigues of his colleagues. Yet the governor was able to make a brave start, and before he had finished he had firmly laid the foundations of French trading supremacy in these western regions.

During the first three years after his coming to Canada, the governor had ruled alone. There was no intendant or bishop to hamper him, for both Talon and Laval had gone to France in 1672. But in 1675 Laval returned to the colony, and in the same year a new intendant, Jacques Duchesneau, was appointed. With this change in the situation at Quebec the friction began in earnest, for Frontenac's imperious temper did not make him a cheerful sharer of authority with any one else. If the intendant and the bishop had been men of conflicting ideas and dispositions, Frontenac might easily have held the balance of power; but they were men of kindred aims, and they readily combined against the governor. United in their opposition to him, they were together a fair match for Frontenac in ability and astuteness. It was not long, accordingly, before the whole colony was once more aligned in two factions. With the governor were the merchants, many of the seigneurs, and all the *coureurs-de-bois*. Supporting the intendant and the bishop were many of the subordinate officials, all of the priests, and those of the tradesmen and habitants with whom the clerical influence was paramount.

The story of the quarrels which went on between these two factions during the years 1675–1680 is neither brief nor edifying. The root of it all lay in the governor's western policy, his encouragement of the forest traders or *coureurs-de-bois*, and his connivance at the use of brandy in the Indian trade. There were unseemly squabbles about precedence at council meetings and at religious festivals, about trivialities of every sort; but the question of the brandy trade was at the bottom of them all. The bishop flayed the governor for letting this trade go on; the missionaries declared that it was proving the ruin of their efforts; and the intendant declared that Frontenac allowed it to continue because he was making a personal profit from the traffic. Charges and counter-charges went home to France with every ship. The intendant wrote dispatches of wearisome length, rehearsing the governor's usurpations, insults, and incompetence. "Disorder," he told the minister, "rules everywhere. Universal confusion prevails; justice is openly perverted, and violence supported by authority determines everything." In language quite as unrestrained Frontenac recounted in detail the difficulties with which he had to contend owing to the intendant's obstinacy, intrigue, and dishonesty. The minister, appalled by the bewildering contradictions, could only lay the whole matter before the King, who determined to try first a courteous reprimand and to that end sent an autograph letter to each official. Both letters were alike in admonishing the governor and the intendant to work in harmony for the good of the colony, but each concluded with the significant warning: "Unless you harmonize better in the future than in the past, my only alternative will be to recall you both."

This intimation, coming straight from their royal master, was to each a rebuke which could not be misunderstood. But it did not accomplish much, for the bitterness and jealousy existing between the two colonial officers was too strong to be overcome. The very next vessels took to France a new budget of complaints and recriminations from both. The King, as good as his word, issued prompt orders for their recall and the two officials left for home, but not on the same vessel, in the summer of 1682.

The question as to which of the two was the more at fault is hardly worth determining. The share of blame to be cast on each by the verdict of history should probably be about equal. Frontenac was by far the abler man, but he had the defects of his qualities. He could not brook the opposition of men less competent than he was, and when he was provoked his arrogance became intolerable. In broader domains of political action he would soon have out-generaled his adversary, but in these petty fields of neighborhood bickering Duchesneau, particularly with the occasional nudgings which he received from Laval, proved no unequal match. The fact remains that neither was able or willing to sacrifice personal animosities nor to display any spirit of cordial coöperation even at the royal command. The departure of both was regarded as a blessing by the majority of the colonists to whom the continued squabbles had become wearisome. Yet there was not lacking, in the minds of many among them, the conviction that if ever again New France should find itself in urgent straits, if ever there were critical need of an iron hand to rule within and to guard without, there would still be one man whom, so long as he lived, they could confidently ask to be sent out to them again. For the time being, however, Frontenac's official career seemed to be at an end. At sixty-two he could hardly hope to regain the royal favor by further service. He must have left the shores of New France with a heavy heart.

Frontenac's successor was La Barre, an old naval officer who had proved himself as capable at sea as he was now to show himself incompetent on land. He was the antithesis of his headstrong predecessor, weak in decision, without personal energy, without imagination, but likewise without any of Frontenac's skill in the art of making enemies. With La Barre came Meulles, an abler and more energetic colleague, who was to succeed Duchesneau as intendant. Both reached Quebec in the autumn of 1682, and problems in plenty they found awaiting them. Shortly before their arrival a fire had swept through the settlement at Quebec, leaving scarcely a building on the lands below the cliff. To make matters worse, the Iroquois had again thrown themselves across the western trade route and had interrupted the coming of the colony's fur supply. As every one now recognized that the protection of this route was essential, La Barre decided that the Iroquois must be taught a lesson. Preparations in rather ostentatious fashion were therefore made for a punitive expedition, and in the summer of 1684 the governor with his troops was at Cataraqui. At this point, however, he began to question whether a parley might not be a better means of securing peace than the laying waste of Indian lands. Accordingly, it was arranged that a council with the Iroquois should be held across the lake from Cataraqui at a place which later took the name of La Famine from the fact that during the council the French supplies ran low and the troops had to be put on short rations.

After negotiations which the cynical chronicler La Hontan has described with picturesque realism, an inglorious truce was patched up. The new governor was sadly deficient in his knowledge of the Indian temperament. He had given the Iroquois an impression that the French were too proud to fight. For their part the Iroquois offered him war or peace as he might choose, and La Barre assured them that he chose to live at peace. When the expedition returned to Quebec there was great disgust throughout the colony, the echoes of which were not without their effect at Versailles, and La Barre was forthwith recalled.

In his place the King sent out the Marquis de Denonville in 1685 with power to make war on the tribesmen or to respect the peace as he might find expedient upon his arrival. The new governor was an honest, well-intentioned soul, neither mentally incapable nor lacking in personal courage. He might have served his King most acceptably in many posts of routine officialdom, but he was not the man to handle the destinies of half a continent in critical years. His mission, to be sure, was no sinecure, for the Iroquois had grown bolder with the assurance of support from the English. Now that they were securing arms and ammunition from Albany it was probable that they would carry their raids right to the heart of New France. Denonville was therefore forced to the conclusion that he had better strike quickly. In making this decision he was right, for in dealing with the Indians a thrust was almost always the best defense.

Armed preparations were consequently once more placed under way, and in the summer of 1687 a flotilla of canoes and batteaux bearing soldiers and supplies was again at Cataraqui. This time the expedition was stronger in numbers and better equipped than ever before. Down the lakes from Michilimackinac came a force of *coureurs-de-bois*, among them seasoned veterans of the wilderness like Du Lhut, Tonty, La Forêt, Morel de la Durantaye, and Nicholas Perrot, each worth a whole squad of soldiers when it came to fighting the Iroquois in their own forests. At the rendezvous across the lake from Cataraqui the French and their allies mustered nearly three thousand men. Denonville had none of his predecessor's bravado coupled with cowardice; his plans were carried forward with a precision worthy of Frontenac. Unlike Frontenac, however, he had a scant appreciation of the skill with which the red man could get out of the way in the face of danger, By moving too slowly after he had set out overland towards the Seneca villages, he gave the enemy time to place themselves out of his reach. So he burned their villages and destroyed large areas of growing corn. After more than a week had been spent in laying waste the land, Denonville and his expedition retired slowly to Cataraqui. Leaving part of his force there, the governor went westward to Niagara, where he rebuilt in more substantial fashion La Salle's old fort at that point and placed it in charge of a garrison. The *coureurs-de-bois* then continued on their way to Michilimackinac while Denonville returned to Montreal.

The expedition of 1687 had not been a fiasco like that of 1685, but neither was it in any real way a success. It angered the whole Iroquois confederacy without having sufficiently impressed the Indians with the punitive power of the French. Denonville had stirred up the nest without destroying the hornets. It was all too soon the Indians' turn to show what they could do as ravagers of unprotected villages; within a year after the French expedition had returned, the Iroquois bands were raiding the territory of the French to the very outskirts of Montreal itself. The route to the west was barred; the fort at Niagara had to be abandoned; Cataraqui was cut off from succor and ultimately had to be destroyed by its garrison; not a single canoe-load of furs came down from the lakes during the entire summer. The merchants were facing ruin, and the whole colony was beginning to tremble for its very existence. The seven years since Frontenac left the land had indeed been a lurid interval.

It was at this juncture that tidings of the colony's dire distress were hurried to the King, and the Grand Monarch moved with rare good sense. He promptly sent for that grim old veteran whom he had recalled in anger seven years before. In all the realm Frontenac was the one man who could be depended upon to restore the prestige of France along the great trade routes.

The Great Onontio, as Frontenac was known to the Indians, reached the St. Lawrence in the late autumn of 1689, just as the colony was about to pass through its darkest hours. Quebec greeted him as a *Redemptor Patriae;* its people, in the words of La Hontan, were as Jews welcoming the Messiah.

Nor was their enthusiasm without good cause, for in a few years Frontenac demonstrated his ability to put the colony on its feet once more. He settled its internal broils, opened the channels of trade, restored the forts, repulsed the English, and brought the Iroquois to terms.

Now that his mission had been achieved and he was no longer as robust as of old, the Iron Governor asked the minister to keep him in mind for some suitable sinecure in France if the opportunity came. This the minister readily promised, but the promise was still unfulfilled when Frontenac was stricken with his last illness. On November 28, 1698, the greatest of the Onontios, or governors, passed away. "Devoted to the service of his king," says his eulogist, "more busied with duty than with gain; inviolable in his fidelity to his friends, he was as vigorous a supporter as he was an untiring foe." Had his official career closed with his recall in 1682, Frontenac would have ranked as one of the singular misfits of the old French colonial system. But the brilliant successes of his second term made men forget the earlier days of petulance and petty bickerings. In the sharp contrasts of his nature Frontenac was an unusual man, combining many good and great qualities with personal shortcomings that were equally pronounced. In the civil history of New France he challenges attention as the most remarkable figure.

CHAPTER VI

THE greatest and most enduring achievement of Frontenac's first term was the exploration of the territory southwestward of the Great Lakes and the planting of French influence there. This work was due, in large part, to the courage and energy of the intrepid La Salle. René-Robert Cavelier, Sieur de La Salle, like so many others who followed the fleur-de-lis into the recesses of the new continent, was of Norman birth and lineage. Rouen was the town of his nativity; the year 1643 probably the date of his birth. How the days of his youth were spent we do not know except that he received a good education, presumably in a Jesuit seminary. While still in the early twenties he came to Montreal where he had an older brother, a priest of the Seminary of St. Sulpice. This was in 1666. Through the influence of his brother, no doubt, he received from the Seminary a grant of the seigneury at Lachine on the river above the town, and at once began the work of developing this property.

If La Salle intended to become a yeoman of New France, his choice of a site was not of the best. The seigneury which he acquired was one of the most dangerous spots in the whole colony, being right in the path of Iroquois attack. He was able to gather a few settlers around him, it is true, but their homes had to be enclosed by palisades, and they hardly dared venture into the fields unarmed. Though the Iroquois and the French were just now at peace, the danger of treachery was never absent. On the other hand no situation could be more favorable for one desiring to try his hand at the fur trade. It was inevitable, therefore, that a young man of La Salle's adventurous temperament and commercial ancestry should soon forsake the irksome drudgery of clearing land for the more exciting and apparently more profitable pursuit of forest trade. That was what happened. In the winter of 1668–1669 he heard from the Indians their story of a great southwestern river which made its way to the "Vermilion Sea." The recital quickened the restless strain in his Norman blood. Here, he thought, was the long-sought passage to the shores of the Orient, and he determined to follow the river.

Having no other means of obtaining funds with which to equip an expedition, La Salle sold his seigneury and at once began his preparations. In July, 1669, he set off with a party of about twenty men, some of whom were missionaries sent by the Seminary of St. Sulpice to carry the tidings of the faith into the heart of the continent. Up the St. Lawrence and along the south shore of Lake Ontario they went, halting at Irondequoit Bay while La Salle and a few of his followers went overland to the Seneca villages in search of guides. Continuing to Niagara, the party divided and the Sulpicians made their way to the Sault Ste. Marie, while La Salle with the remainder of the expedition struck out south of Lake Erie and in all probability reached the Ohio by descending one of its branches. But, as no journal or contemporary record of the venture after they had left Niagara has come down to us, the details of the journey are unknown. It is believed that desertions among his followers prevented further progress and that, in the winter of 1669–1670, La Salle retraced his steps to the lakes. In its main object the expedition had been a failure.

Having exhausted his funds, La Salle had no opportunity, for the present at least, of making another trial. He accordingly asked Frontenac for trading privileges at Cataraqui, the site of modern Kingston, where stood the fortified post named after the governor. Upon Frontenac's recommendation La Salle received in 1674 not only the exclusive right to trade but also a grant of land at Fort Frontenac on condition that he would rebuild the defenses with stone and supply a garrison. The conditions being acceptable, the explorer hastened to his new post and was soon engaged in the fur trade upon a considerable scale. La Salle, however, needed more capital than he himself could supply, and in 1677 he made a second trip to France with letters from Frontenac to the King and Colbert. He also had the further design in view of obtaining authority and funds for another trip of exploration to the West. Since his previous expedition in 1669 two of his compatriots, Père Marquette and Louis Joliet, had reached the Great River and had found every reason for believing that its course ran south to the Gulf of Mexico, and not southwestward to the Gulf of California, as had previously been supposed. But they had not followed the Mississippi to its outlet, and this was what La Salle was now determined to do.

In Paris he found attentive listeners to his plans, and even the King's ministers were interested, so that when La Salle sailed back to Quebec in 1678 he brought a royal decree authorizing him to proceed with his project. With him came a daring spirit who was to be chief lieutenant and faithful companion in the ensuing years, Henri de Tonty. This adventurous soldier was later known among the Indians as "Tonty of the Iron Hand," for in his youth he had lost a hand in battle, and in its stead now wore an artificial one of iron, which he used from time to time with wholesome effect. He was a man of great physical strength and commensurate courage, loyal to his chief and almost La Salle's equal in perseverance.

La Salle's party lost no time in proceeding to Fort Frontenac. Even though the winter was at hand, Hennepin was at once sent forward to Niagara with instructions to build a post and to begin the construction of a vessel so that the journey westward might be begun with the opening of spring. Later in the winter La Salle and Tonty joined the party at Niagara where the fort was completed. Before spring arrived, a vessel of about forty-five tons, the largest yet built for service on the lakes, had been constructed. On its prow stood a carved griffin, from the armorial bearings of Frontenac, and out of its portholes frowned several small cannon. With the advent of summer La Salle and his followers went aboard; the sails were spread, and in due course the expedition reached Michilimackinac, where the Jesuits had already established their most westerly mission.

The arrival of the *Griffin* brought Indians by the hundred to marvel at the "floating fort" and to barter their furs for the trinkets with which La Salle had provided himself. The little vessel then sailed westward into Lake Michigan and finally dropped anchor in Green Bay where an additional load of beaver skins was put on deck. With the approach of autumn the return trip began. La Salle, however, did not accompany his valuable cargo, having a mind to spend the winter in explorations along the Illinois. In September, with many misgivings, he watched the *Griffin* set sail in charge of a pilot. Then, with the rest of his followers he started southward along the Wisconsin shore. Reaching the mouth of the St. Joseph, he struck into the interior to the upper

Kankakee. This stream the voyageurs, who numbered about forty in all, descended until they reached the Illinois, which they followed to the point where Peoria now stands.

Here La Salle's troubles began in abundance. The Indians endeavored to dissuade him from leading the expedition farther, and even the explorer's own followers began to desert. Chagrinned at these untoward circumstances and on his guard lest the Indians prove openly hostile, La Salle proceeded to secure his position by the erection of a fort to which he gave the name Crèvecœur. Here he left Tonty with the majority of the party, while he himself started with five men back to Niagara. His object was in part to get supplies for building a vessel at Fort Crèvecœur, and in part to learn what had become of the *Griffin*, for since that vessel had sailed homeward he had heard no word from her crew. Proceeding across what is now southern Michigan, La Salle emerged on the shores of the Detroit River. From this point he pushed across the neck of land to Lake Erie, where he built a canoe which brought him to Niagara at Eastertide, 1680. His fears for the fate of the *Griffin* were now confirmed: the vessel had been lost, and with her a fortune in furs. Nothing daunted, however, La Salle hurried on to Fort Frontenac and thence with such speed to Montreal that he accomplished the trip from the Illinois to the Ottawa in less than three months—a feat hitherto unsurpassed in the annals of American exploration.

At Montreal the explorer, who once more sought the favor of Frontenac, was provided with equipment at the King's expense. Within a few months he was again at Fort Frontenac and ready to rejoin Tonty at Crèvecœur. Just as he was about to depart, however, word came that the Crèvecœur garrison had mutinied and had destroyed the post. La Salle's one hope now was that his faithful lieutenant had held on doggedly and had saved the vessel he had been building. But Tonty in the meantime had made his way with a few followers to Green Bay, so that when La Salle reached the Illinois he found everyone gone. Undismayed by this climax to his misfortunes, La Salle nevertheless pushed on down the Illinois, and early in December reached its confluence with the Mississippi.

To follow the course of this great stream with the small party which accompanied him seemed, however, too hazardous an undertaking. La

Salle, therefore, retraced his steps once more and spent the next winter at Fort Miami on the St. Joseph to the southeast of Lake Michigan. In the spring word came to him that Tonty was at Michilimackinac, and thither he hastened, to hear from Tonty's own lips the long tale of disaster. "Any one else," wrote an eye-witness of the meeting, "would have thrown up his hands and abandoned the enterprise; but far from this, with a firmness and constancy that never had its equal, I saw him more resolved than ever to continue his work and push forward his discovery."

Now that he had caught his first glimpse of the Mississippi, La Salle was determined to persist until he had followed its course to the outlet. Returning with Tonty to Fort Frontenac, he replenished his supplies. In this same autumn of 1681, with a larger number of followers, the explorer was again on his way to the Illinois. By February the party had reached the Mississippi. Passing the Missouri and the Ohio, La Salle and his followers kept steadily on their way and early in April reached the spot where the Father of Waters debouches through three channels into the Gulf. Here at the outlet they set up a column with the insignia of France, and, as they took possession of the land in the name of their King, they chanted in solemn tones the *Exaudiat*, and in the name of God they set up their banners.

But the French were short of supplies and could not stay long after the symbols of sovereignty had been raised aloft. Paddling slowly against the current, La Salle and his party reached the Illinois only in August. Here La Salle and Tonty built their Fort St. Louis and here they spent the winter. During the next summer (1683) the indefatigable explorer journeyed down to Quebec, and on the last ship of the year took passage for France. In the meantime, Frontenac, always his firm friend and supporter, had been recalled, and La Barre, the new governor, was unfriendly. A direct appeal to the home authorities for backing seemed the only way of securing funds for further explorations.

Accordingly, early in 1684 La Salle appeared at the French court with elaborate plans for founding a colony in the valley of the lower Mississippi. This time the expedition was to proceed by sea. To this project the King gave his assent, and commanded the royal officers to furnish the supplies. By midsummer four ships were ready to set sail for the Gulf. Once more, however, troubles beset La Salle on every hand. Disease broke out on the vessels; the officers quarreled among themselves; the expedition was attacked by the Spaniards, and one ship was lost. Not until the end of December was a landing made, and then not at the Mississippi's mouth but at a spot far to the west of it, on the sands of Matagorda Bay.

Finding that he had missed his reckonings, La Salle directed a part of his company to follow the shore. After many days of fruitless search they established a permanent camp and sent the largest vessel back to France. Their repeated efforts to reach the Mississippi overland were in vain. Finally, in the winter of 1687, La Salle with a score of his strongest followers struck out northward, determined to make their way to the Lakes, where they might find succor. To follow the detail of their dreary march would be tedious. The hardships of the journey, without adequate equipment or provisions, and the incessant danger of attack by the Indians increased petty jealousies into open mutiny. On the 19th of March, 1687, the courageous and indefatigable La Salle was treacherously assassinated by one of his own party. Here in the fastnesses of the Southwest died at the age of forty-four the intrepid explorer of New France, whom Tonty called—perhaps not untruthfully—"one of the greatest men of this age."

"Thus," writes a later historian with all the perspective of the intervening years, "was cut short the career of a man whose personality is impressed in some respects more strongly than that of any other upon the history of New France. His schemes were too far-reaching to succeed. They required the strength and resources of a half-dozen nations like the France of Louis XIV. Nevertheless the lines upon which New France continued to develop were substantially those which La Salle had in mind, and the fabric of a wilderness empire, of which he laid the foundations, grew with the general growth of colonization, and in the next century became truly formidable. It was not until Wolfe climbed the Heights of Abraham that the great ideal of La Salle was finally overthrown."

It would be difficult, indeed, to find among the whole array of explorers which history can offer in all ages a perseverance more dogged in the face of abounding difficulties. Phœnix-like, he rose time after time from the ashes of adversity. Neither fatigue nor famine, disappointment nor even disaster, availed to swerve him from his purpose. To him, more than to any one else of his time, the French could justly attribute their early hold upon the great regions of the West. Other explorers and voyageurs of his generation there were in plenty, and their service was not inconsiderable. But in courage and persistence, as well as in the scope of his achievements, La Salle, the pathfinder of Rouen, towered above them all. He had, what so many of the others lacked, a clear vision of what the great plains and valleys of the Middle West could yield towards the enrichment of a nation in years to come. "America," as Parkman has aptly said, "owes him an enduring memory; for in this masculine figure she sees the pioneer who guided her to the possession of her richest heritage."

CHAPTER VII

NEARLY all that was distinctive in the life of old
Canada links itself in one way or another with
the Catholic religion. From first to last in the
history of New France the most pervading trait
was the loyalty of its people to the church of their
fathers. Intendants might come and go; governors abode their destined hour and went their way;
but the apostles of the ancient faith never for one
moment released their grip upon the hearts and
minds of the Canadians. During two centuries
the political life of the colony ran its varied
rounds; the habits of the people were transformed
with the coming of material prosperity; but the
Church went on unchanged, unchanging. One
may praise the steadfastness with which the
Church fought for what its bishops believed to be
right, or one may, on the other hand, decry the
arrogance of its pretensions to civil power and its

hampering conservatism; but as the great central fact in the history of New France, the hegemony of Catholicism cannot be ignored.

When Frenchmen began the work of founding a dominion in the New World, their own land was convulsed with religious troubles. Not only were the Huguenots breaking from the confines of the old religion, but within the Catholic Church itself in France there were two great contending factions. One group strove for the preservation of the Gallican liberties, the special rights of the French King and the French bishops in the ecclesiastical government of the land, while the other claimed for the Pope a supremacy over all earthly rulers in matters of spiritual concern. It was not a difference on points of doctrine, for the Gallicans did not question the headship of the Papacy in things of the spirit. What they insisted upon was the circumscribed nature of the papal power in temporal matters within the realm of France, particularly with regard to the right of appointment to ecclesiastical positions with endowed revenues. Bishops, priests, and religious orders ranged themselves on one side or the other, for it was a conflict in which there could be no neutrality. As the royal authorities were heart and soul with the Gallicans, it was natural enough that priests of this group should gain the first religious foothold in the colony. The earliest priests brought to the colony were members of the Récollet Order. They came with Champlain in 1615, and made their headquarters in Quebec at the suggestion of the King's secretary. For ten years they labored in the colony, striving bravely to clear the way for a great missionary crusade.

But the day of the Récollets in New France was not long. In 1625 came the advance guard of another religious order, the militant Jesuits, bringing with them their traditions of unwavering loyalty to the Ultramontane cause. The work of the Récollets had, on the whole, been disappointing, for their numbers and their resources proved too small for effective progress. During ten years of devoted labor they had scarcely been able to make any impression upon the great wilderness of heathenism that lay on all sides. In view of the apparent futility of their efforts, the coming of the Jesuits — suggested, it may be, by Champlain — was probably not unwelcome to them. Richelieu, moreover, had now brought his Ultramontane sympathies close to the seat of royal power, so that the King no longer was in a position to oppose the project. At any rate the Jesuits sailed for Canada, and their arrival forms a notable landmark in the history of the colony. Their dogged zeal and iron persistence carried them to points which missionaries of no other religious order would have reached. For the Jesuits were, above all things else, the harbingers of a militant faith. Their organization and their methods admirably fitted them to be the pioneers of the Cross in new lands. They were men of action, seeking to win their crown of glory and their reward through intense physical and spiritual exertions, not through long seasons of prayer and meditation in cloistered seclusion. Loyola, the founder of the Order, gave to the world the nucleus of a crusading host, disciplined as no army ever was. If the Jesuits could not achieve the spiritual conquest of the New World, it was certain that no others could. And this conquest they did achieve. The whole course of Catholic missionary effort throughout the Western Hemisphere was shaped by members of the Jesuit Order.

Only four of these priests came to Quebec in 1625. Although it was intended that others should follow at once, their number was not substantially increased until seven years later, when the troubles with England were brought to an end and the colony was once more securely in the hands of the French. Then the Jesuits came steadily, a few arriving with almost every ship, and either singly or together they were sent off to the Indian settlements — to the Hurons around the Georgian Bay, to the Algonquins north of the Ottawa, and to the Iroquois south of the Lakes. The physical vigor, the moral heroism, and the unquenchable religious zeal of these missionaries were qualities exemplified in a measure and to a degree which are beyond the power of any pen to describe. Historians of all creeds have tendered homage to their self-sacrifice and zeal, and never has work of human hand or spirit been more worthy of tribute. The Jesuit went, often alone, where no others dared to go, and he faced unknown dangers which had all the possibilities of torture and martyrdom. Nor did this energy waste itself in flashes of isolated triumph. The Jesuit was a member of an efficient organization, skillfully guided by inspired leaders and carrying its extensive work of Christianization with machine-like thoroughness through the vastness of five continents. We are

too apt to think only of the individual missionary's glowing spirit and rugged faith, his picturesque strivings against great odds, and to regard
him as a guerilla warrior against the hosts of
darkness. Had he been this, and nothing more
his efforts must have been altogether in vain. The
great services which the Jesuit missionary rendered
in the New World, both to his country and to his
creed, were due not less to the matchless organization of the Order to which he belonged than to
qualities of courage, patience, and fortitude which
he himself showed as a missionary.

During the first few years of Jesuit effort
among the Indians of New France the results
were pitifully small. The Hurons, among whom
the missionaries put forth their initial labors
were not the best of prospective converts. The
minds of these half-nomadic peoples, to the white
man, were filled with gross superstitions and their
senses had been brutalized by the incessant tor-
ments of their Iroquois enemies. Amid the toils
and hazards and discomforts of so insecure and
wandering a life the Jesuits found little opportunity for soundly instructing the Hurons in the
faith. Hence there were but few neophytes in
these early years. By 1640 the missionaries could

count only a hundred converts in a population of
many thousands, and even this little quota
included many infants who had died soon after
receiving the rites of baptism. More missionaries kept coming, however; the work steadily
broadened; and the posts of service were multi-
plied. In due time the footprints of the Jesuits
were everywhere, from the St. Lawrence to the
Mississippi, from the tributaries of the Hudson
to the regions north of the Ottawa. Le Jeune,
Massé, Brébeuf, Lalemant, Ragueneau, Le
Dablon, Jogues, Garnier, Raymbault, Péron,
Moyne, Allouez, Druilletes, Chaumonot, Ménard,
Bressani, Daniel, Chabanel, and a hundred others,
—they soon formed that legion whose works of courage and devotion stand forth so prominently in the
early annals of New France.

Once at their stations in the upper country, the
missionaries regularly sent down to the Superior
of the Order at Quebec their full reports of
progress, difficulties, and hopes, all mingled with
interesting descriptions of Indian customs, folklore, and life. It is no wonder that these narra-
tives, "jotted down hastily," as Le Jeune tells us,
"now in one place, now in another, sometimes on
water, sometimes on land," were often crude, or

that they required careful editing before being
sent home to France for publication. In their
printed form, however, these *Rélations des Jésuites*
gained a wide circle of European readers; they
inspired more missionaries to come, and they
drew from well-to-do laymen large donations
of money for carrying on the crusade.

The royal authorities also gave their earnest
support, for they saw in the Jesuit missionary not
merely a torchbearer of his faith or a servant of the
Church. They appreciated his loyalty and remembered that he never forgot his King, nor shirked
his duty to the cause of France among the tribes.
Every mission post thus became an embassy,
and every Jesuit an ambassador of his race, striving to strengthen the bonds of friendship between
the people to whom he went and the people from
whom he came. The French authorities at Quebec were not slow to recognize what an ever-
present help the Jesuit could be in times of Indian
trouble. One governor expressed the situation
with fidelity when he wrote to the home authorities that, "although the interests of the Gospel do
not require us to keep missionaries in all the Indian
villages, the interests of the civil government for
the advantage of trade must induce us to manage

things so that we may always have at least one of
them there." It must therefore be admitted that,
when the civil authorities did encourage the
missions, they did not always do so with a purely
spiritual motive in mind.

As the political and commercial agent of his
people, the Jesuit had great opportunities, and
in this capacity he usually gave a full measure of
service. After he had gained the confidence of the
tribes, the missionary always succeeded in getting
the first inkling of what was going on in the way
of inter-tribal intrigues. He learned to fathom
the Indian mind and to perceive the Indian's
motives. He was thus able to communicate to
Quebec the information and advice which so often
helped the French to outwit their English rivals.
As interpreters in the conduct of negotiations and
the making of treaties the Jesuits were also in-
valuable. How much, indeed, these blackrobes
achieved for the purely secular interests of the
French colony, for its safety from sudden Indian
attack, for the development of its trade, and for
its general upbuilding, will never be known. The
missionary did not put these things on paper,
but he rendered services which in all probability
were far greater than posterity will ever realize.

It was not, however, with the conversion of the
Indians or with the service of French secular
interests among the Indians that the work of the
Jesuits was wholly, or even chiefly, concerned.
During the middle years of the seventeenth century, these services at the outposts of French
territory may have been most significant, for the
French population along the shores of the St.
Lawrence remained small, the settlements were
closely huddled together, and a few priests could
serve their spiritual needs.   The popular impression of Jesuit enterprises in the New World is
connected almost wholly with work among the
Indians.   This pioneer phase of the Jesuit's work
was picturesque, and historians have had a great
deal to say about it.   It was likewise of this service
in the depths of the interior that the missionary
himself wrote most frequently.   But as the colony
grew and broadened its bounds until its settlements stretched all the way from the Saguenay to
Montreal and beyond, a far larger number of
curés was needed.   Before the old régime came to
a close there were far more Frenchmen than
Indians within the French sphere of influence
in America, and they required by far the greater
share of Jesuit ministration, and, long before the

old dominion ended, the Indian missions had to take a subordinate place in the general program of Jesuit undertakings. The outposts in the Indian country were the chief scene of Jesuit labors from 1615 to about 1700, when the emphasis shifted to the St. Lawrence valley. Some of the mission fields held their own to the end, but in general they failed to make much headway during the last half-century of French rule. The Church in the settled portions of the colony, however, kept on with its steady progress in achievement and power.

New France was the child of missionary fervor. Even from the outset, in the scattered settlements along the St. Lawrence, the interests of religion were placed on a strictly missionary basis. There were so-called parishes in the colony almost from its beginning, but not until 1722 was the entire colony set off into recognized ecclesiastical parishes, each with a fixed *curé* in charge. Through all the preceding years each village or *côte* had been served by a missionary, by a movable *curé*, or by a priest sent out from the Seminary at Quebec. No priest was tied to any parish but was absolutely at the immediate beck and call of the bishop. Some reason for this unsettled arrangement might be found in the conditions under which the colony developed in its early years, with its sparse population ranging far and wide, with its lack of churches and of *presbytères* in which the priest might reside. But the real explanation of its long continuance lies in the fact that, if regular *curés* were appointed, the seigneurs would lay claim to various rights of nomination or patronage, whereas the bishop could control absolutely the selection of missionary priests and could thus more easily carry through his policy of ecclesiastical centralization.

Not only in this particular, but in every other phase of religious life and organization during these crusading days in Canada, one must reckon not only with the logic of the situation, but also with the dominating personality of the first and greatest Ultramontane, Bishop Laval. Though not himself a Jesuit, for no member of the Order could be a bishop, Laval was in tune with their ideals and saw eye to eye with the Jesuits on every point of religious and civil policy.

François-Xavier de Laval, Abbé de Montigny, was born in 1622, a scion of the great house of Montmorency. He was therefore of high nobility, the best-born of all the many thousands who came

to New France throughout its history.   As a youth
he had come into close association with the
Jesuits, and had spent four years in the famous
Hermitage at Caen, that Jesuit stronghold which
served so long as the nursery for the spiritual
pioneers of early Canada.   When he came to
Quebec as Vicar-Apostolic in 1659, he was only
thirty-seven years of age.   His position in the
colony at the time of his arrival was somewhat
unusual, for although he was to be in command
of the colony's spiritual forces, New France was
not yet organized as a diocese and could not
be so organized until the Pope and the King
should agree upon the exact status of the Church
in the French colonial dominions.   Laval was
nevertheless given his titular rank from the ancient
see of Petræa in Arabia which had long since been
in partibus infidelium and hence had no bishop
within its bounds.   From his first arrival in
Canada he was Bishop Laval, but without a
diocese over which he could actually hold sway.
His commission as Vicar-Apostolic gave him
power enough, however, and his responsibility
was to the Pope alone.

For the tasks which he was sent to perform,
Laval had eminent qualifications.   A haughty

spirit went with the ultra-blue blood in his veins;
he had a temperament that loved to lead and to
govern, and that could not endure to yield or
to lag behind. His intellectual talents were high
beyond question, and to them he added the blessing of a rugged physical frame. No one ever
came to a new land with more definite ideas of
what he wanted to do or with a more unswerving
determination to do it in his own way.

It was not long before the stamp of Laval's firm
hand was laid upon the life of the colony. In
due course, too, he found himself at odds with
the governor. The dissensions smouldered at
first, and then broke out into a blaze that warmed
the passions of all elements in the colony. The
exact origin of the feud is somewhat obscure,
and it is not necessary to put down here the details
of its development to the war *à outrance* which
soon engaged the civil and ecclesiastical authorities
in the colony. In the background was the question of the *coureurs-de-bois* and the liquor traffic
which now became a definite issue and which
remained the storm centre of colonial politics
for many generations. The merchants insisted
that if this traffic were extinguished it would
involve the ruin of the French hold upon the

Indian trade. The bishop and the priests, on the other hand, were ready to fight the liquor traffic to the end and to exorcise it as the greatest blight upon the New World. Quebec soon became a cockpit where the battle of these two factions raged. Each had its ups and downs, until in the end the traffic remained, but under a makeshift system of regulation.

To portray Laval and his associates as always in bitter conflict with the civil power, nevertheless, would be to paint a false picture. Church and state were not normally at variance in their views and aims. They clashed fiercely on many occasions, it is true, but after their duels they shook hands and went to work with a will at the task of making the colony stand upon its own feet. Historians have magnified these bickerings out of all proportion. Squabbles over matters of precedence at ceremonies, over the rate of the tithes, and over the curbing of the *coureurs-de-bois* did not take the major share of the Church's attention. For the greater part of two whole centuries it loyally aided the civil power in all things wherein the two could work together for good.

And these ways of assistance were many. For example the Church, through its various institutions and orders, rendered a great service to colonial agriculture. As the greatest landowner in New France, it set before the seigneurs and the habitants an example of what intelligent methods of farming and hard labor could accomplish in making the land yield its increase. The King was lavish in his grants of territory to the Church: the Jesuits received nearly a million *arpents* as their share of the royal bounty; the bishop and the Quebec Seminary, the Sulpicians, and the Ursulines, about as much more. Of the entire granted acreage of New France the Church controlled about one-quarter, so that its position as a great landowner was even stronger in the colony than at home. Nor did it fold its talents in a napkin. Colonists were brought from France, farms were prepared for them in the church seigneuries, and the new settlers were guided and encouraged through the troublous years of pioneering. With both money and brains at its command, the Church was able to keep its own lands in the front line of agricultural progress.

When in 1722 the whole colony was marked off into definite ecclesiastical divisions, seventy-two parishes were established, and nearly one hundred *curés* were assigned to them. As time went on, both parishes and *curés* increased in number, so that every locality had its spiritual leader who was also a philosopher and guide in all secular matters. The priest thus became a part of the community and never lost touch with his people. The habitant of New France for his part never neglected his Church on week-days. The priest and the Church were with him at work and at play, the spirit and the life of every community. Though paid a meager stipend, the *curé* worked hard and always proved a laborer far more than worthy of his hire. The clergy of New France never became a caste, a privileged order; they did not live on the fruits of other men's labor, but gave to the colony far more than the colony ever gave to them.

As for the Church revenues, these came from several sources. The royal treasury contributed large sums, but, as it was not full to overflowing, the King preferred to give his benefactions in generous grants of land. Yet the royal subsidies amounted to many thousand livres each year. The diocese of Quebec was endowed with the revenues of three French abbeys. Wealthy laymen in France followed the royal example and sent contributions from time to time, frequently of large amount. While the Company of One Hundred Associates controlled the trade of the colony, it made from its treasury some provisions for the support of the missionaries. After 1663, a substantial source of ecclesiastical income was the tithe, an ecclesiastical tax levied annually upon all produce of the land, and fixed in 1663 at one-thirteenth. Four years later it was reduced to one-twenty-sixth, and Bishop Laval's strenuous efforts to have the old rate restored were never successful.

In education, yet another field of colonial life, the Church rendered some service. Here the civil authorities did nothing at all, and had it not been for the Church the whole colony would have grown up in absolute illiteracy. A school for boys was established at Quebec in Champlain's day, and during the next hundred and fifty years it was followed by about thirty others. More than a dozen elementary schools for girls were also established under ecclesiastical auspices. Yet the amount of secular education imparted by all these seminaries was astoundingly small, and they did but little to leaven the general illiteracy of the population. Only the children of the towns attended the schools, and the program of study was of the most elementary character. Religious instruction was given the first place and received so much attention that there was little time in school hours for anything else. The girls fared better than the boys on the whole, for the nuns taught them to sew and to knit as well as to read and to write.

So far as secular education was concerned, therefore, the English conquest found the colony in almost utter stagnation. Not one in five hundred among the habitants, it was said, could read or write. Outside the immediate circle of clergy, officials, and notaries, ignorance of even the rudiments of education was almost universal. There were no newspapers in the colony and very few books save those used in the services of worship. Greysolon Du Lhut, the king of the voyageurs, for example, was a man of means and education, but his entire library, as disclosed by his will, consisted of a world atlas and a set of Josephus. The priests did not encourage the reading of secular books, and La Hontan recounts the troubles which he had in keeping one militant *curé* from tearing his precious volumes to pieces. New France was at that period not a land where freedom dwelt with knowledge.

Intellectually, the people of New France comprised on the one hand a small élite and on the other a great unlettered mass. There was no middle class between. Yet the population of the colony always contained, especially among its officials and clergy, a sprinkling of educated and scholarly men. These have given us a literature of travel and description which is extensive and of high quality. No other American colony of the seventeenth and eighteenth centuries put so much of its annals into print; the *Rélations* of the Jesuits alone were sufficient to fill forty-one volumes, and they form but a small part of the entire literary output.

CHAPTER VIII

FROM the beginning of the colony there ran in the minds of French officialdom the idea that the social order should rest upon a seigneurial basis. Historians have commonly attributed to Richelieu the genesis of New World feudalism, but without good reason, for its beginnings antedated the time of the great minister. The charter issued to the ill-starred La Roche in 1598 empowered him "to grant lands to gentlemen in the forms of fiefs and seigneuries," and the different viceroys who had titular charge of the colony before the Company of One Hundred Associates took charge in 1627 had similar powers. Several seigneurial grants in the region of Quebec had, in fact, been made before Richelieu first turned his attention to the colony.

Nor was the adoption of this policy at all unnatural. Despite its increasing obsolescence,

the seigneurial system was still strong in France
and dominated the greater part of the kingdom.
The nobility and even the throne rested upon it.
The Church, as suzerain of enormous landed
estates, sanctioned and supported it. The masses
of the French people were familiar with no other
system of landholding. No prolonged quest need
accordingly be made to explain why France
transplanted feudalism to the shores of the great
Canadian waterway; in fact, an explanation
would have been demanded had any other policy
been considered. No one asks why the Puritans
took to Massachusetts Bay the English system
of freehold tenure. They took the common law
of England and the tenure that went with it.
Along with the fleur-de-lis, likewise, went the
Custom of Paris and the whole network of social
relations based upon a hierarchy of seigneurs and
dependents.

The seigneurial system of land tenure, as all
students of history know, was feudalism in a
somewhat modernized form. During the chaos
which came upon Western Europe in the centuries
following the collapse of Roman imperial supremacy, every local magnate found himself forced
to depend for existence upon the strength of his

own castle, under whose walls he gathered as many vassals as he could induce to come. To these he gave the surrounding lands free from all rents, but on condition of aid in time of war. The lord gave the land and promised to protect his vassals, who, on their part, took the land and promised to pay for it not in money or in kind, but in loyalty and service. Thus there was created a close personal relation, a bond of mutual wardship and fidelity which bound liegeman and lord with hoops of steel. The whole social order rested upon this bond and upon the gradations in privilege which it involved in a sequence which became stereotyped. In its day feudalism was a great institution and one which shared with the Christian Church the glory of having made mediæval life at all worth living. It helped to keep civilization from perishing utterly in a whirl of anarchy, and it enabled Europe to recover inch by inch its former state of order, stability, and law.

But, having done its service to humanity, feudalism did not quietly make way for some other system more suited to the new conditions. It hung on grimly long after the forces which had brought it into being ceased to exist, long after the growth of a strong monarchy in France with a

powerful standing army had removed the necessity
of mutual guardianship and service.   To meet the
new conditions the system merely changed its
incidents, never its general form.   The ancient
obligation of military service, no longer needed,
gave place to dues and payments.   The old
personal bond relaxed; the feudal lord became
the seigneur, a mere landlord.   The vassal became
the *censitaire*, a mere tenant, paying heavy dues
each year in return for protection which he no
longer received nor required.   In a word, before
160U the feudal system had become the seigneurial
system, and it was the latter which was established
in the French colony of Canada.

In the new land there was reason to hope, however, that this system of social relations based
upon landholding would soon work its way back
to the vigor which it had displayed in mediæval
days.   Here in the midst of an unfathomed wilderness was a small European settlement with hostile
tribes on every hand.   The royal arm, so strong
in affording protection at home, could not strike
hard and promptly in behalf of subjects a thousand leagues away.   New France, accordingly
must organize itself for defense and repel her
enemies just as the earldoms and duchies of the

crusading centuries had done. And that is just what the colony did, with the seigneurial system as the groundwork of defensive strength. Under stress of the new environment, which was not wholly unlike that of the former feudal days, the military aspects of the system revived and the personal bond regained much of its ancient vigor. The sordid phases of seigneurialism dropped into the background. It was this restored vitality that helped, more than all else, to turn New France into a huge armed camp which hordes of invaders, both white and red, strove vainly to pierce time after time during more than a full century.

The first grant of a seigneury in the territory of New France was made in 1623 to Louis Hébert, a Paris apothecary who had come to Quebec with Champlain some years before this date. His land consisted of a tract upon the height above the settlement, and here he had cleared the fields and built a home for himself. By this indenture feudalism cast its first anchor in New France, and Hébert became the colony's first patron of husbandry. Other grants soon followed, particularly during the years when the Company of One Hundred Associates was in control of the land, for, by the terms of its charter, this organization was empowered to grant large tracts as seigneuries and also to issue patents of nobility. It was doubtless assumed by the King that such grants would be made only to persons who would actually emigrate to New France and who would thus help in the upbuilding of the colony, but the Company did not live up to this policy. Instead, it made lavish donations, some of them containing a hundred square miles or more, to directors and friends of the Company in France who neither came to the colony themselves nor sent representatives to undertake the clearing of these large estates. One director took the entire Island of Orleans; others secured generous slices of the best lands on both shores of the St. Lawrence; but not one of them lifted a finger in the way of redeeming these huge concessions from a state of wilderness primeval. The tracts were merely held in the hope that some day they would become valuable. Out of sixty seigneuries which were granted by the Company during the years from 1632 to 1663 not more than a half-dozen grants were made to *bona fide* colonists. At the latter date the total area of cleared land was scarcely four thousand *arpents.*[1]

[1] An *arpent* was about five-sixths of an acre.

With the royal action of 1663 which took the colony from the Company and reconstructed its government, the seigneurial system was galvanized at once with new energy. The uncleared tracts which the officials of the Company had carved out among themselves were declared to be forfeited to the Crown and actual occupancy was held to be, for the future, the essential of every seigneurial grant. A vigorous effort was made to obtain settlers, and with considerable success, for in the years 1665–1667 the population of the colony more than doubled. Nothing was left undone by the royal authorities in securing and transporting emigrants. Officials from Paris scoured the provinces, offering free passage to Quebec and free grants of land upon arrival. The campaign was successful, and many shiploads of excellent colonists, most of them hardy peasants from Normandy, Brittany, Perche, and Picardy, were sent during these banner years.

On their arrival at Quebec the incoming settlers were taken in hand by officials and were turned over to the various seigneurs who were ready to provide them with lands and to help them in getting well started. If the newcomer happened to be a man of some account at home, and particu-

larly if he brought some money with him, he had
the opportunity to become a seigneur himself.
He merely applied to the intendant, who was
quite willing to endow with a seigneury any one
who appeared likely to get it cleared and ready for
future settlers.   In this matter the officials, following out the spirit of the royal orders, were prone
to err on the side of liberality.   Too often they
gave large seigneurial grants to men who had
neither the energy nor the funds to do what was
expected of a seigneur in the new land.

As for extent, the seigneuries varied greatly.
Some were as large as a European dukedom; others
contained only a few thousand *arpents*.   There
was no fixed rule; within reasonable limits each
applicant obtained what he asked for, but it
was generally understood that men who had been
members of the French *noblesse* before coming
to the colony were entitled to larger areas than
those who were not.   In any case little attention
was paid to exact boundaries, and no surveys
were made.   In making his request for a seigneury
each applicant set forth what he wanted, and this
he frequently did in such broad terms as, "all lands
between such-and-such a river and the seigneury
of the Sieur de So-and-So."   These descriptions,

rarely adequate or accurate, were copied into the patent, causing often hopeless confusion of boundaries and unneighborly squabbles. It was fortunate that most seigneurs had more land than they could use; otherwise there would have been as many lawsuits as seigneuries.

The obligations imposed upon the seigneurs were not burdensome. No initial payment was asked, and there were no annual rentals to be paid to the Crown. Each seigneur had to render the ceremony of fealty and homage to the royal representative at Quebec. Each was liable for military service, although that obligation was not written into the grant. When a seigneury changed owners otherwise than by inheritance in direct succession, a payment known as the *quint* (being, as the name connotes, one-fifth of the reported value) became payable to the royal treasury, but this was rarely collected. The most important obligation imposed upon the Canadian seigneur, and one which did not exist at all in France, was that of getting settlers established upon his lands. This obligation the authorities insisted upon above all others. The Canadian seigneur was expected to live on his domain, to gather dependents around him, to build a mill for grinding

their grain, to have them level the forest, clear the
fields, and make two blades of grass grow where
one grew before.   In other words, the Canadian
seigneur was to be a royal immigration and land
agent combined.   He was not given his generous
landed patrimony in order that he should sit
idly by and wait for the unearned increment to
come.

Many of the seigneurs fulfilled this trust to the
letter.   Robert Giffard, who received the seigneury of Beauport just below Quebec, was one of
these; Charles Le Moyne, Sieur de Longueuil,
was another.   Both brought many settlers from
France and saw them safely through the years of
pioneering.   Others, however, did no more than
flock to Quebec when ships were expected, like
so many real estate agents explaining to the new
arrivals what they had to offer in the way of
lands fertile and well situated.   Still others did
not even do so much, but merely put forth one
excuse after another to explain why their tracts
remained without settlements at all.   From time
to time the authorities prodded these seigneurial
drones and threatened them with the forfeiture
of their estates; but some of the laggards had
friends among the members of the Sovereign

Council or possessed other means of warding off action, so that final decrees of forefeiture were rarely issued. Occasionally there were seigneurs whose estates were so favorably situated that they could exact a bonus from intending settlers, but the King very soon put a stop to this practice. By the Arrêts of Marly in 1711 he decreed that no bonus or *prix d'entrée* should be exacted by any seigneur, but that every settler was to have land for the asking and at the rate of the annual dues customary in the neighborhood.

At this date there were some ninety seigneuries in the colony, about which we have considerable information owing to a careful survey which was made in 1712 at the King's request. This work was entrusted to an engineer, Gedéon de Catalogne, who had come to Quebec a quarter of a century earlier to help with the fortifications. Catalogne spent two years in his survey, during which time he visited practically all the colonial estates. As a result he prepared and sent to France a full report giving in each case the location and extent of the seigneury, the name of its owner, the nature of the soil, and its suitability for various uses, the products, the population, the condition of the people, the provisions made for religious instruc-

tion, and various other matters.[1]   With the report
he sent three maps, one of which has disappeared
The others show the location of all seigneuries in
the regions of Quebec and Three Rivers.

From Catalogne's survey we know that before
1712 nearly all the territory on both shores of the
St. Lawrence from below Quebec to above Montreal had been parceled into seigneuries.   Likewise
the islands in the river and the land on both sides
of the Richelieu in the region toward Lake Champlain had been allotted.   Many of the seigneuries
in this latter belt had been given to officers of the
Carignan-Salières regiment which had come out
with Tracy in 1665 to chastise the Mohawks
After the work of the regiment had been finished
Talon suggested to the King that it be disbanded
in Canada, that the officers be persuaded to accept
seigneuries, and that the soldiers be given lands
within the estates of their officers.   The Grand
Monarque not only assented but promised a liberal
money bonus to all who would remain.   Accord
ingly, more than twenty officers, chiefly captains
or lieutenants, and nearly four hundred men

[1] This report was printed for the first time in the author'
Documents relating to the Seigniorial Tenure in Canada (Toronto
The Champlain Society, 1908).

agreed to stay in New France under these arrangements.

Here was an experiment in the system of imperial Rome repeated in the New World. When the empire of the Cæsars was beginning to give way before the oncoming Goths and Huns, the practice of disbanding the legions on the frontier so that they might settle there and form an iron ring against the invaders was adopted and served its purpose for a time. It was from these *prædia militaria* that Talon got the idea which he now transmitted to the French King with the suggestion that "the practice of these sagacious and warlike Romans might be advantageously followed in a land which, being so far away from its sovereign, must trust for existence to the strength of its own arms." In keeping with the same precedent, Talon located the military seigneuries in that section of the colony where they would be most useful as a barrier against the enemy; that is to say, he placed them in the colony's most vulnerable region. This was the area along the Richelieu from Lake Champlain to its confluence with the St. Lawrence at Sorel. It was by this route that the Mohawks had already come more than once on their errands of massacre, and it was by

this portal that the English were likely to come
if they should ever attempt to overwhelm New
France by an overland assault. The region of the
Richelieu was therefore made as strong against
incursion as this colonizing measure could make
it.

All who took lands in this region, whether
seigneurs or habitants, were to assemble in arms at
the royal call. Their uniforms and muskets they
kept for service, and never during subsequent
years was such a call without response. These military settlers and their sons after them were only
too ready to rally around the royal *oriflamme* at any
opportunity. It was from the armed seigneuries
of the Richelieu that Hertel de Rouville, St. Ours,
and others quietly slipped forth and leaped with
all the advantage of surprise upon the lonely hamlets of outlying Massachusetts or New York. How
the English feared these *gentilshommes* let their
own records tell, for there these French colonials
put many a streak of blood and fire.

But not all of the seigneuries were settled in this
way, and it was well for the best interests of the
colony that they were not. Too often the good
soldier made only an indifferent yeoman. First in
war, he was last in peace. The task of hammer-

ing spears into ploughshares and swords into pruning-hooks was not altogether to his liking. Most of the officers gradually grew tired of their rôle as gentlemen of the wilderness, and eventually sold or mortgaged their seigneuries and made their way back to France. Many of the soldiers succumbed to the lure of the western fur traffic and became *coureurs-de-bois*. But many others stuck valiantly to the soil, and today their descendants by the thousand possess this fertile land.

What were the obligations of the settler who took a grant of land within a seigneury? On the whole they were neither numerous nor burdensome, and in no sense were they comparable with those laid upon the hapless peasantry in France during the days before the great Revolution. Every habitant had a written title-deed from his seigneur and the terms of this deed were explicit. The seigneur could exact nothing that was not stipulated therein. These title-deeds were made by the notaries, of whom there seem to have been plenty in New France; the census of 1681 listed no fewer than twenty-four of them in a population which had not yet reached ten thousand. When the deed had been signed, the notary gave one copy to each of the parties; the original he kept himself. These scribes were men of limited education and did not always do their work with proper care, but on the whole they rendered useful service.

The deed first set forth the situation and area of the habitant's farm. The ordinary extent was from one hundred to four hundred *arpents*, usually in the shape of a parallelogram with a narrow frontage on the river, and extending inland to a much greater distance. Everyone wanted to be near the main road which ran along the shore; it was only after all this land had been taken up that the incoming settlers were willing to have farms in the "second range" on the uplands away from the stream. At any rate, the habitant took his land subject to yearly payments known as the *cens et rentes*. The amount was small, a few sous together with a stated donation in grain or poultry to be delivered each autumn. Reckoned in terms of present-day rentals, the *cens et rentes* amounted to half a dozen chickens or a bushel of grain for each fifty or sixty acres of land. Yet this was the only payment which the habitants of New France regularly made in return for their lands. Each autumn at Michaelmas they gathered at the seigneur's house, their carryalls filling his yard. One by one they handed over their quota of grain or poultry and counted out their *cens* in copper coins. The occasion became a neighborhood festival to which the women came with the men. There was a general retailing of local gossip and a squaring-up of accounts among the neighbors themselves.

But while this was the only regular payment made by the habitant, it was not the only obligation imposed upon him. In New France the seigneur had the exclusive right of grinding all grain, and the habitants were bound by their title-deeds to bring their grist to his mill and to pay the legal toll for milling. This *banalité*, as it was called, did not bear heavily upon the people; most of the complaints concerning it came rather from the seigneurs who claimed that the legal toll, which amounted to one-fourteenth of the grain, did not suffice to pay expenses. Some of the seigneurs did not build mills at all, but the authorities eventually moved them to action by ordering that those who did not provide mills at once would not be allowed to enforce the obligation of toll at any future date. Most of the seigneurial mills were crude, wind-driven affairs which made poor flour and often kept the habitants waiting for days to get it. Usually built in tower-like fashion, they were loopholed in order to afford places of refuge and defense against Indian attack.

Another seigneurial obligation was that of giving to the seigneur certain days of *corvée*, or forced labor, in each year. In France this was a grievous burden; peasants were taken from their own lands at inconvenient seasons and forced to work for weeks on the seigneur's domain. But there was nothing of this sort in Canada. The amount of *corvée* was limited to six days at the most in any year, of which only two days could be asked for at seed-time and two days at harvest. The seigneur, for his part, did not usually exact even this amount, because the neighborhood custom required that he should furnish both food and tools to those whom he called upon to work for him.

Besides, there were various details of a minor sort incidental to the seigneurial system. If the habitant caught fish in the river, one fish in every eleven belonged to the seigneur. But seldom was any attention paid to this stipulation. The seigneur was entitled to take firewood and building materials from the lands of his habitants if he desired, but he rarely availed himself of this right. On the morning of every May Day the habitants were under strict injunction to plant a Maypole before the seigneur's house, and this they never failed to do, because the seigneur in return was expected to dispense hospitality to all who came. Bright and early in the morning the whole community appeared and greeted the seigneur with a salvo of blank musketry. With them they carried a tall fir-tree, pulled bare to within a few feet of the top where a tuft of green remained. Having planted this Maypole in the ground, they joined in dancing and a *feu de joie* in the seigneur's honor, and then adjourned for cakes and wine at his table. There is no doubt that such good things disappeared with celerity before appetites whetted by an hour's exercise in the clear spring air. After drinking to the seigneur's health and to the health of all his kin, the merry company returned to their homes, leaving behind them the pole as a souvenir of their homage. That the seigneur was more than a mere landlord such an occasion testified.

The seigneurs of New France had the right to hold courts for the settlement of disputes among their tenantry, but they rarely availed themselves

of this privilege because, owing to the sparseness
of the population in most of the seigneuries, the
fines and fees did not produce enough income to
make such a procedure worth while. In a few
populous districts there were seigneurial courts
with regular judges who held sessions once or
twice each week. In some others the seigneur
himself sat in judgment behind the living-room
table in his own home and meted out justice after
his own fashion. The Custom of Paris was
the common law of the land, and all were supposed to know its provisions, though few save
the royal judges had any such knowledge. When
the seigneur himself heard the suitors, his decision
was not always in keeping with the law but it
usually satisfied the disputants, so that appeals
to the royal courts were not common. These
latter tribunals, each with a judge of its own, sat
at Quebec, Three Rivers, and Montreal. Their
procedure, like that of the seigneurial courts,
was simple, free from chicane, and inexpensive.
A lawsuit in New France did not bring ruinous
costs. "I will not say," remarks the facetious La
Hontan, "that the Goddess of Justice is more
chaste here than in France, but at any rate, if she
is sold, she is sold more cheaply. In Canada we

do not pass through the clutches of advocates, the talons of attorneys, and the claws of clerks. These vermin do not as yet infest the land.   Every one here pleads his own cause.   Our Themis is prompt, and she does not bristle with fees, costs, and charges."

Throughout the French period there was no complaint from the habitants concerning the burdens of the seigneurial tenure.   Here and there disputes arose as to the exact scope and nature of various obligations, but these the intendant adjusted with a firm hand and an eye to the general interest.   On the whole, the system rendered a highly useful service, by bringing the entire rural population into close and neighborly contact, by affording a firm foundation for the colony's social structure, and by contributing greatly to the defensive unity of New France.   So long as the land was weak and depended for its very existence upon the solidarity of its people, so long as the intendant was there to guide the system with a prætorian hand and to prevent abuses, so long as strength was more to be desired than opulence, the seigneurial system served New France better than any other scheme of landholding would have done.   It was only when the administration

of the country came into new and alien hand
that Canadian seigneurialism became a barrier t
economic progress and an obsolete system whic
had to be abolished.

CHAPTER IX

THE COUREURS-DE-BOIS

THE center and soul of the economic system in New France was the traffic in furs. Even before the colony contained more than a handful of settlers, the profit-making possibilities of this trade were recognized. It grew rapidly even in the early days, and for more than a hundred and fifty years furnished New France with its sinews of war and peace. Beginning on the St. Lawrence, this trade moved westward along the Great Lakes, until toward the end of the seventeenth century it passed to the headwaters of the Mississippi. During the two administrations of Frontenac the fur traffic grew to large proportions, nor did it show much sign of shrinking for a generation thereafter. With the ebb-tide of French military power, however, the trader's hold on these western lands began to relax, and before the final overthrow of New France it had become greatly weakened.

In establishing commercial relations with the Indians, the French voyageur on the St. Lawrence had several marked advantages over his English and Dutch neighbors. By temperament he was better adapted than they to be a pioneer of trade. No race was more supple than his own in conforming its ways to the varied demands of place and time. When he was among the Indians, the Frenchman tried to act like one of them, and he soon developed in all the arts of forest life a skill which rivaled that of the Indian himself. The fascination of life in the untamed wilderness with its hair-raising experiences, its romance, its free abandon, appealed more strongly to the French temperament than to that of any other European race. *Non licet omnibus adire Corinthum.* And the French colonist of the seventeenth century had the qualities of personal courage and hardihood which enabled him to enjoy this life to the utmost.

Then there was the Jesuit missionary. He was the first to visit the Indians in their own abodes, the first to make his home among them, the first to master their language and to understand their habits of mind. This sympathetic comprehension gave the Jesuit a great influence

n the councils of the Indians. While first of
all a soldier of the Cross, the missionary never
forgot, however, that he was also a sentinel doing
outpost duty for his own race. Apostle he was,
but patriot too. Besides, it was to the spiritual
interest of the missionary to keep his flock in
contact with the French alone; for if they became
acquainted with the English they would soon come
under the smirch of heresy. To prevent the Indians from engaging in any commercial dealings
with Dutch or English heretics meant encouraging
them to trade exclusively with the French. In
this way the Jesuit became one of the most zealous
of helpers in carrying out the French program
for diverting to Montreal the entire fur trade of
the western regions. He was thus not only a pioneer of the faith but at the same time a pathfinder
of commercial empire. It is true, no doubt, that this
service to the trading interests of the colony was
but ill-requited by those whom it benefited most.
The trader too often repaid the missionary in
pretty poor coin by bringing the curse of the liquor
traffic to his doors, and by giving denial by shameless conduct to all the good father's moral teachings. In spite of such inevitable drawbacks, the
Jesuit rendered a great service to the trading

interests of New France, far greater indeed than he ever claimed or received credit for.

In the struggle for the control of the fur trade geographical advantages lay with the French. They had two excellent routes from Montreal directly into the richest beaver lands of the continent. One of these, by way of the Ottawa and Mattawa rivers, had the drawback of an overland portage, but on the other hand the whole route was reasonably safe from interruption by Iroquois or English attack. The other route, by way of the upper St. Lawrence and the lakes, passed Cataraqui, Niagara, and Detroit on the way to Michilimackinac or to Green Bay. This was an all-water route, save for the short detour around the falls at Niagara, but it had the disadvantage of passing, for a long stretch, within easy reach of Iroquois interference. The French soon realized, however, that this lake route was the main artery of the colony's fur trade and must be kept open at any cost. They accordingly entrenched themselves at all the strategic points along the route. Fort Frontenac at Cataraqui was built in 1674; the fortified post at Detroit, in 1686; the fort at Niagara, in 1678; and the establishments at the Sault Ste. Marie and at

Michilimackinac had been constructed even earlier.

But these places only marked the main channels through which the trade passed. The real sources of the fur supply were in the great regions now covered by the states of Ohio, Wisconsin, Iowa, and Minnesota. As it became increasingly necessary that the French should gain a firm footing in these territories as well, they proceeded to establish their outposts without delay. The post at Baye des Puants (Green Bay) was established before 1685; then in rapid succession came trading stockades in the very heart of the beaver lands, Fort St. Antoine, Fort St. Nicholas, Fort St. Croix, Fort Perrot, Fort St. Louis, and several others. No one can study the map of this western country as it was in 1700 without realizing what a strangle-hold the French had achieved upon all the vital arteries of its trade.

The English had no such geographical advantages as the French, nor did they adequately appreciate the importance of being first upon the ground. With the exception of the Hudson after 1664, they controlled no great waterway leading to the interior. And the Hudson with its tributaries tapped only the territories of the Iroquois which were denuded of beaver at an early date. These Iroquois might have rendered great service to the English at Albany by acting as middlemen in gathering the furs from the West. They tried hard, indeed, to assume this rôle, but, as they were practically always at enmity with the western tribes, they never succeeded in turning this possibility to their full emolument.

In only one respect were the French at a serious disadvantage. They could not compete with the English in the matter of prices. The English trader could give the Indian for his furs two or three times as much merchandise as the French could offer him. To account for this commercial discrepancy there were several reasons. The cost of transportation to and from France was high— approximately twice that of freighting from London to Boston or New York. Navigation on the St. Lawrence was dangerous in those days before buoys and beacons came to mark the shoal waters, and the risk of capture at sea during the incessant wars with England was considerable. The staples most used in the Indian trade— utensils, muskets, blankets, and strouds (a coarse woolen cloth made into shirts)—could be bought more cheaply in England than in France. Rum could be obtained from the British West Indies more cheaply than brandy from across the ocean. Moreover, there were duties on furs shipped from Quebec and on all goods which came into that post. And, finally, a paternal government in New France set the scale of prices in such a way as to ensure the merchants a large profit. It is clear, then, that in fair and open competition for the Indian trade the French would not have survived a single season.[1] Their only hope was to keep the English away from the Indians altogether, and particularly from the Indians of the fur-bearing regions. This was no easy task, but in general they managed to do it for nearly a century.

The most active and at the same time the most picturesque figure in the fur-trading system of New France was the *coureur-de-bois*. Without him the trade could neither have been begun nor

[1] In the collection of *Documents Relating to the Colonial History of New York* (ix., 408–409) the following comparative table of prices at Fort Orange (Albany) and at Montreal in 1689 is given:

The Indian pays for	at Albany		at Montreal	
1 musket	2	beavers	5	beavers
8 pounds of powder	1	beaver	4	"
40 pounds of lead	1	"	3	"
1 blanket	1	"	2	"
4 shirts	1	"	2	"
6 pairs stockings	1	"	2	"

continued successfully. Usually a man of good birth, of some military training, and of more or less education, he was a rover of the forest by choice and not as an outcast from civilization. Young men came from France to serve as officers with the colonial garrison, to hold minor civil posts, to become seigneurial landholders, or merely to seek adventure. Very few came out with the fixed intention of engaging in the forest trade; but hundreds fell victims to its magnetism after they had arrived in New France. The young officer who grew tired of garrison duty, the young seigneur who found yeomanry tedious, the young habitant who disliked the daily toil of the farm — young men of all social ranks, in fact, succumbed to this lure of the wilderness. "I cannot tell you," wrote one governor, "how attractive this life is to all our youth. It consists in doing nothing, caring nothing, following every inclination, and getting out of the way of all restraint." In any case the ranks of the voyageurs included those who had the best and most virile blood in the colony.

Just how many Frenchmen, young and old, were engaged in the lawless and fascinating life of the forest trader when the fur traffic was at its height cannot be stated with exactness. But the number

must have been large. The intendant Duchesneau, in 1680, estimated that more than eight
hundred men, out of a colonial population numbering less than ten thousand, were off in the woods.
"There is not a family of any account," he wrote
to the King, "but has sons, brothers, uncles, and
nephews among these *coureurs-de-bois*." This
may be an exaggeration, but from references
contained in the dispatches of various royal officials
one may fairly conclude that Duchesneau's esti-
mate of the number of traders was not far wide
of the mark. And there is other evidence as to the
size of this exodus to the woods. Nicholas Perrot,
when he left Montreal for Green Bay in 1688,
took with him one hundred and forty-three
voyageurs.[1] La Hontan found "thirty or forty
coureurs-de-bois at every post in the Illinois
country."[2]

Among the leaders of the *coureurs-de-bois*
several names stand out prominently. François
Dauphine de la Forêt, Nicholas Perrot, and Henri
de Tonty, the lieutenants of La Salle, Alphonse de
Tonty, Antoine de La Mothe-Cadillac, Greysolon
Du Lhut and his brother Greysolon de la Tourette,

[1] *Documents Relative to the Colonial History of New York*, ix., 470.
[2] *Voyages* (ed. Thwaites), ii., 175.

Pierre Esprit Radisson and Médard Chouart de Groseilliers, Olivier Morel de la Durantaye, Jean-Paul Le Gardeur de Repentigny, Louis de la Porte de Louvigny, Louis and Juchereau Joliet, Pierre Le Sueur, Boucher de la Perrière, Jean Peré, Pierre Jobin, Denis Massé, Nicholas d'Ailleboust de Mantet, François Perthuis, Etienne Brulé, Charles Juchereau de St. Denis, Pierre Moreau *dit* La Toupine, Jean Nicolet — these are only the few who connected themselves with some striking event which has transmitted their names to posterity. Many of them have left their imprint upon the geographical nomenclature of the Middle West. Hundreds of others, the rank and file of this picturesque array, gained no place upon the written records, since they took part in no striking achievement worthy of mention in the dispatches and memoirs of their day. The *coureur-de-bois* was rarely a chronicler. If the Jesuits did not deign to pillory him in their *Relations*, or if the royal officials did not single him out for praise in the memorials which they sent home to France each year, the *coureur-de-bois* might spend his whole active life in the forest without transmitting his name or fame to a future generation. And that is what most of them did. A few of the voyageurs found that one trip to the wilds was enough and never took to the trade permanently. But the great majority, once the virus of the free life had entered their veins, could not forsake the wild woods to the end of their days. The dangers of the life were great, and the mortality among the traders was high. *Coureurs de risques* they ought to have been called, as La Hontan remarks. But taken as a whole they were a vigorous, adventurous, strong-limbed set of men. It was a genuine compliment that they paid to the wilderness when they chose to spend year after year in its embrace.

In their methods of trading the *coureurs-de-bois* were unlike anything that the world had ever known before. The Hanseatic merchants of earlier fur-trading days in Northern Europe had established their forts or factories at Novgorod, at Bergen, and elsewhere, great *entrepôts* stored with merchandise for the neighboring territories. The traders lived within, and the natives came to the posts to barter their furs or other raw materials. The merchants of the East India Company had established their posts in the Orient and traded with the natives on the same basis. But the Norman voyageurs of the New World did things quite differently. They established fortified posts throughout the regions west of the Lakes, it is true, but they did not make them storehouses, nor did they bring to them any considerable stock of merchandise. The posts were for use as the headquarters of the *coureurs-de-bois*, and usually sheltered a small garrison of soldiers during the winter months; they likewise served as places of defense in the event of attack and of rendezvous when a trading expedition to Montreal was being organized. It was not the policy of the French authorities, nor was it the plan of the *coureurs-de-bois*, that any considerable amount of trading should take place at these western stockades. They were only the outposts intended to keep the trade running in its proper channels. In a word, it was the aim of the French to bring the trade to the colony, not to send the colony overland to the Indians. That is the way Father Carheil phrased it, and he was quite right.[1]

Every spring, accordingly, if the great trade routes to Montreal were reasonably free from the danger of an overwhelming Iroquois attack, the *coureurs-de-bois* rounded up the western Indians

[1] Carheil to Champigny (August 30, 1702), in R. G. Thwaites, *Jesuit Relations and Allied Documents*, lxv., 219.

with their stocks of furs from the winter's hunt.
Then, proceeding to the grand rendezvous at
Michilimackinac or Green Bay, the canoes were
joined into one great flotilla, and the whole array
set off down the lakes or by way of the Ottawa
to Montreal. This annual fur flotilla often
numbered hundreds of canoes, the *coureurs-de-
bois* acting as pilots, assisting the Indians to ward
off attacks, and adding their European intelligence
to the red man's native cunning.[1] About midsummer, having covered the thousand miles of
water, the canoes drew within hail of the settlement of Montreal. Above the Lachine Rapids
the population came forth to meet it with a noisy
welcome. Enterprising *cabaretiers*, in defiance
of the royal decrees, had usually set up their
booths along the shores for the sale of brandy,
and there was some brisk trading as well as a
considerable display of aboriginal boisterousness
even before the canoes reached Montreal.

Once at the settlement, the Indians set up their
tepees, boiled their kettles, and unpacked their
bundles of peltry. A day was then given over to a

---

[1] The flotilla of 1693 consisted of more than 400 canoes, with about
200 *coureurs-de-bois*, 1200 Indians, and furs to the value of over
800,000 *livres*.

great council which the governor of the colony, in scarlet cloak and plumed hat, often came from Quebec to attend.   There were the usual pledges of friendship; the peace-pipe went its round, and the song of the calumet was sung.   Then the trading really began.   The merchants of Montreal had their little shops along the shore where they spread out for display the merchandise brought by the spring ships from France.   There were muskets, powder, and lead, blankets in all colors, coarse cloth, knives, hatchets, kettles, awls, needles, and other staples of the trade.   But the Indian had a weakness for trinkets of every sort, so that cheap and gaudy necklaces, bracelets, tin looking-glasses, little bells, combs, vermilion, and a hundred other things of the sort were there to tempt him.   And last, but not least in its purchasing power, was brandy.   Many hogsheads of it were disposed of at every annual fair, and while it lasted the Indians turned bedlam loose in the town.   The fair was Montreal's gala event in every year, for its success meant everything to local prosperity.   Indeed, in the few years when, owing to the Iroquois dangers, the flotilla failed to arrive, the whole settlement was on the verge of bankruptcy.

What the Indian got for his furs at Montreal varied from time to time, depending for the most part upon the state of the fur market in France. And this, again, hinged to some extent upon the course of fashions there. On one occasion the fashion of wearing low-crowned hats cut the value of beaver skins in two. Beaver was the fur of furs, and the mainstay of the trade. Whether for warmth, durability, or attractiveness in appearance, there was none other to equal it. Not all beaver skins were valued alike, however. Those taken from animals killed during the winter were preferred to those taken at other seasons, while new skins did not bring as high a price as those which the Indian had worn for a time and had thus made soft. The trade, in fact, developed a classification of beaver skins into soft and half-soft, green and half-green, wet and dry, and so on. Skins of good quality brought at Montreal from two to four *livres* per pound, and they averaged a little more than two pounds each. The normal cargo of a large canoe was forty packs of skins, each pack weighing about fifty pounds. Translated into the currency of today a beaver pelt of fair quality was worth about a dollar. When we read in the official dispatches that a half-million *livres'* worth of skins changed owners at the Montreal fair, this statement means that at least a hundred thousand animals must have been slaughtered to furnish a large flotilla with its cargo.

The furs of other animals, otter, marten, and mink, were also in demand but brought smaller prices. Moose hides sold well, and so did bear skins. Some buffalo hides were brought to Montreal, but in proportion to their value they were bulky and took up so much room in the canoes that the Indians did not care to bring them. The heyday of the buffalo trade came later, with the development of overland transportation. At any rate the dependence of New France upon these furs was complete. "I would have you know," asserts one chronicler, "that Canada subsists only upon the trade of these skins and furs, three-fourths of which come from the people who live around the Great Lakes." The prosperity of the French colony hinged wholly upon two things: whether the routes from the West were open, and whether the market for furs in France was holding up. Upon the former depended the quantity of furs brought to Montreal; upon the latter, the amount of profit which the *coureurs-*

de-bois and the merchants of the colony would obtain.

For ten days or a fortnight the great fair at Montreal continued. A picturesque bazaar it must have been, this meeting of the two ends of civilization, for trade has been, in all ages, a mighty magnet to draw the ends of the earth together. When all the furs had been sold, the *coureurs-de-bois* took some goods along with them to be used partly in trade on their own account at the western posts and partly as presents from the King to the western chieftains. There is reason to suspect, however, that much of what the royal bounty provided for this latter purpose was diverted to private use. There were annual fairs at Three Rivers for the Indians of the St. Maurice region; at Sorel, for those of the Richelieu; and at Quebec and at Tadoussac, for the redskins of the Lower St. Lawrence. But Montreal, owing to its situation at the confluence of the St. Lawrence and Ottawa trade routes, was by far the greatest fur mart of all.

It has been mentioned that the colonial authorities tried to discourage trading at the western posts. Their aim was to bring the Indian with his furs to the colonial settlement. But this policy could not be fully carried out. Despite the most rigid prohibitions and the severest penalties, some of the *coureurs-de-bois* would take goods and brandy to sell in the wilderness. Finding that this practice could not be exterminated, the authorities decided to permit a limited amount of forest trading under strict regulation, and to this end the King authorized the granting of twenty-five licenses each year. These licenses permitted a trader to take three canoes with as much merchandise as they would hold. As a rule the licenses were not issued directly to the traders themselves, but were given to the religious institutions or to dependent widows of former royal officers. These in turn sold them to the traders, sometimes for a thousand *livres* or more. The system of granting twenty-five annual licenses did not of itself throw the door wide open for trade at the western establishments. But as time went on the plan was much abused by the granting of private licenses to the friends of the officials at Quebec, and "God knows how many of these were issued," as one writer of the time puts it. Traders often went, moreover, without any license at all, and especially in the matter of carrying brandy into the forest they frequently set the official orders at defiance.

This brandy question was, in fact, the great troubler in Israel. It bulks large in every chronicle, every memoir, every *Rélation*, and in almost every official dispatch during a period of more than fifty years. It worried the King himself; it set the officers of the Church and State against each other; and it provoked more friction throughout the western dominions of France than all other issues put together.

As to the ethics of the liquor traffic in New France, there was never any serious disagreement. Even the secular authorities readily admitted that brandy did the Indians no good, and that it would be better to sell them blankets and kettles. But that was not the point. The traders believed that, if the western Indians could not secure brandy from the French, they would get rum from the English. The Indian would be no better off in that case, and the French would lose their hold on him into the bargain. Time and again they reiterated the argument that the prohibition of the brandy trade would make an end to trade, to French influence, and even to the missionary's own labors. For if the Indian went to the English for rum, he would get into touch with heresy as well; he would have Protestant missionaries come to his village, and the day of Jesuit missionaries would be at an end.

This, throughout the whole trading period, was the stock argument of publicans and sinners. The Jesuit missionaries combated it with all their power; yet they never fully convinced either the colonial or the home authorities. Louis XIV, urged by his confessor to take one stand and by his ministers to take the other, was sorely puzzled. He wanted to do his duty as a Most Christian King, yet he did not want to have on his hands a bankrupt colony. Bishop Laval pleaded with Colbert that brandy would spell the ruin of all religion in the new world, but the subtle minister calmly retorted that the *eau-de-vie* had not yet overcome the ancient church in older lands. To set his conscience right, the King referred the whole question to the savants of the Sorbonne, and they, like good churchmen, promptly gave their opinion that to sell intoxicants to the heathen was a heinous sin. But that counsel afforded the Grand Monarch scant guidance, for it was not the relative sinfulness of the brandy trade that perplexed him. The practical expediency of issuing a decree of prohibition was what lay upon his mind. On that point Colbert gave him sensible advice, namely, that a question of practical policy could be better settled by the colonists themselves than by cloistered scholars. Guided by this suggestion, the King asked for a limited plebiscite; the governor of New France was requested to call together "the leading inhabitants of the colony" and to obtain from each one his opinion in writing. Here was an inkling of colonial self-government, and it is unfortunate that the King did not resort more often to the same method of solving the colony's problems.

On October 26, 1678, Frontenac gathered the "leading inhabitants" in the Château at Quebec. Apart from the officials and military officers on the one hand and the clergy on the other, most of the solid men of New France were there. One after another their views were called for and written down. Most of those present expressed the opinion that the evils of the traffic had been exaggerated, and that if the French should prohibit the sale of brandy to the Indians they would soon lose their hold upon the western trade. There were some dissenters, among them a few who urged a more rigid regulation of the traffic. One hardheaded seigneur, the Sieur Dombourg, raised the query whether the colony was really so dependent for its existence upon the fur trade as the other had assumed to be the case. If there were les attention to trade, he urged, there would be mor heed paid to agriculture, and in the long run i would be better for the colony to ship wheat t France instead of furs. "Let the western trade go to the English in exchange for their rum; i would neither endure long nor profit them much." This was sound sense, but it did not carry great weight with Dombourg's hearers.

The written testimony was put together and with comments by the governor, was sent to France for the information of the King and hi ministers. Apparently it had some effect, for without altogether prohibiting the use of brandy in the western trade, a royal decree of 1679 forbade the *coureurs-de-bois* to carry it with them on thei trips up the lakes. The issue of this decree, how-ever, made no perceptible change in the situation, and brandy was taken to the western posts as before. So far as one can determine from the actual figures of the trade, however, the quantity of intoxicants used by the French in the Indian trade has been greatly exaggerated by the mis-sionaries. Not more than fifty barrels (*barriques*) ever went to the western regions in the course of a year. A barrel held about two hundred and fifty pints, so that the total would be less than one pint per capita for the adult Indians within the French sphere of influence. That was a far smaller per capita consumption than Frenchmen guzzled in a single day at a Breton fair, as La Salle once pointed out. The trouble was, however, that thousands of Indians got no brandy at all, while a relatively small number obtained too much of it. What they got, moreover, was poor stuff, most of it, and well diluted with water. The Indian drank to get drunk, and when brandy constituted the other end of the bargain he would give for it the very furs off his back.

But if the Jesuits exaggerated the amount of brandy used in the trade, they did not exaggerate its demoralizing effect upon both the Indian and the trader. They believed that brandy would wreck the Indian's body and ruin his soul. They were right; it did both. It made of every western post, in the words of Father Carheil, a den of "brutality and violence, of injustice and impiety, of lewd and shameless conduct, of contempt and insults." No sinister motives need be sought to explain the bitterness with which the blackrobes cried out against the iniquities of a system which swindled the Indian out of his furs and debauched him into the bargain. Had the Jesuits done otherwise than fight it from first to last they would have been false to the traditions of their Church and their Order. They were, when all is said and done, the truest friends that the North American Indian has ever had.

The effects of the fur trade upon both Indians and French were far-reaching. The trade changed the red man's order of life, took him in a single generation from the stone to the iron age, demolished his old notions of the world, carried him on long journeys, and made him a different man. French brandy and English rum sapped his stamina, and the *grand libertinage* of the traders calloused whatever moral sense he had. His folklore, his religion, and his institutions made no progress after the trader had once entered his territories.

On the French the effects of tribal commerce were not so disastrous, though pernicious enough. The trade drew off into the wilderness the vigorous blood of the colony. It cast its spell over New France from Lachine to the Saguenay. Men left their farms, their wives, and their families, they mortgaged their property, and they borrowed from their friends in order to join the annual hegira to the West.   Yet very few of these traders accumulated fortunes.   It was not the trader but the merchant at Montreal or Quebec who got the lion's share of the profit and took none of the risks. Many of the *coureurs-de-bois* entered the trade with ample funds and emerged in poverty. Nicholas Perrot and Greysolon Du Lhut were conspicuous examples.   It was a highly speculative game.   At times large profits came easily and were spent recklessly.   The trade encouraged profligacy, bravado, and garishness; it deadened the moral sense of the colony, and even schooled men in trickery and peculation.   It was a corrupting influence in the official life of New France, and even governors could not keep from soiling their hands in it.   But most unfortunate of all, the colony was impelled to put its economic energies into what was at best an ephemeral and transitory source of national wealth and to neglect the solid foundations of agriculture and industry which in the long run would have profited its people much more.

CHAPTER X

AGRICULTURE, INDUSTRY, AND TRADE

IT was the royal desire that New France should
some day become a powerful and prosperous
agricultural colony, providing the motherland
with an acceptable addition to its food supply.
To this end large tracts of land were granted
upon most liberal terms to incoming settlers,
and every effort was made to get these acres
cultivated. Encouragement and coercion were
alike given a trial. Settlers who did well were
given official recognition, sometimes even to the
extent of rank in the *noblesse*. On the other
hand those who left their lands uncleared were
repeatedly threatened with the revocation of
their land-titles, and in some cases their hold-
ings were actually taken away. From the
days of the earliest settlement down to the eve
of the English conquest, the officials of both
the Church and the State never ceased to use

their best endeavors in the interests of colonial agriculture.

Yet with all this official interest and encouragement agricultural development was slow. Much of the land on both the north and the south shores of the St. Lawrence was heavily timbered, and the work of clearing proved tedious. It was estimated that an industrious settler, working by himself, could clear not more than one superficial *arpent* in a whole season. So slowly did the work make progress, in fact, that in 1712, after fifty years of royal paternalism, the cultivable area of New France amounted to only 150,000 *arpents*, and at the close of the French dominion in 1760 it was scarcely more than twice that figure,—in other words, about five *arpents* for each head of population.

While industry and trade, particularly the Indian trade, took the attention and interest of a considerable portion in the population of New France, agriculture was from first to last the vocation of the great majority. The census of 1695 showed more than seventy-five per cent of the people living on the farms of the colony and this ratio was almost exactly maintained, nearly sixty years later, when the census of 1754 was compiled. This population was scattered along both banks of the St. Lawrence from a point well below Quebec to the region surrounding Montreal. Most of the farms fronted on the river so that every habitant had a few *arpents* of marshy land for hay, a tract of cleared upland for ploughing, and an area extending to the rear which might be turned into meadow or left uncleared to supply him with firewood.

Wheat and maize were the great staples, although large quantities of oats, barley, and peas were also grown. The wheat was invariably spring-sown, and the yield averaged from eight to twelve hundredweights per *arpent*, or from ten to fourteen bushels per acre. Most of the wheat was made into flour at the seigneurial mills and was consumed in the colony, but shipments were also made with fair regularity to France, to the West Indies, and for a time to Louisbourg. In 1736 the exports of wheat amounted to nearly 100,000 bushels, and in the year following the banner harvest of 1741 this total was nearly doubled. The price which the habitant got for wheat at Quebec ranged normally from two to four *livres* per hundredweight (about thirty to sixty cents per bushel) depending upon the harvests in the colony and the safety with which wheat could be shipped to France, which, again, hinged upon the fact whether France and England were at peace or at war. Indian corn was not exported to any large extent, but many cargoes of dried peas were sent abroad, and occasionally there were small shipments of oats and beans.

There was also a considerable production of hemp, flax, and tobacco, but not for export in any large quantity. The tobacco grown in the colony was coarse and ill-flavored. It was smoked by both the habitant and the Indian because it was cheap; but Brazilian tobacco was greatly preferred by those who could afford to buy it, and large quantities of this were brought in. The French Government frowned upon tobacco-growing in New France, believing, as Colbert wrote to Talon in 1672, that any such policy would be prejudicial to the interests of the French colonies in the tropical zones which were much better adapted to this branch of cultivation.

Cattle raising made substantial progress, and the King urged the Sovereign Council to prohibit the slaughter of cattle so that the herds might keep on growing; but the stock was not of a high standard, but undersized, of mongrel breed, and poorly cared for. Sheep raising, despite the brisk demand for wool, made slow headway. Most of the wool needed in the colony had to be brought from France, and the demand was great because so much woolen clothing was required for winter use. The keeping of poultry was, of course, another branch of husbandry. The habitants were fond of horses; even the poorest managed to keep two or three, which was a wasteful policy as there was no work for the horses to do during nearly half the year. Fodder, however, was abundant and cost nothing, as each habitant obtained from the flats along the river all that he could cut and carry away. This marsh hay was not of superior quality, but it at least served to carry the horses and stock through the winter.

The methods of agriculture were beyond question slovenly and crude. Catalogne, the engineer whom the authorities commissioned to make an agricultural census of the colony, ventured the opinion that, if the fields of France were cultivated as the farms of Canada were, three-quarters of the French people would starve. Rotation of crops was practically unknown, and fertilization of the land was rare, although the habitant frequently burned the stubble before putting the plough to his fields. From time to time a part of each farm was allowed to lie fallow, but such fallow fields were left unploughed and soon grew so rank with weeds that the soil really got no rest at all. All the ploughing was done in the spring, and it was not very well done at that, for the land was ploughed in ridges which left much waste between the furrows. Too often the seed became poor, as a result of the habitant using seed from his own crops year after year until it became run out. Most of the cultivated land was high and dry and needed no artificial drainage. Even where the water lay on the land late in the spring, however, there was rarely an attempt, as Peter Kalm in his *Travels* remarks, to drain it off. The habitant had patience in greater measure than industry, and he was always ready to wait for nature to do his work. Everybody depended for his implements largely upon his own workmanship, so that the tools of agriculture were of poor construction. The cultivation of even a few *arpents* required a great deal of manual drudgery. On the other hand, the land of New France was fertile, and every one could have plenty of it for the asking. Kalm thought it quite as good as the average in the English colonies and far better than most arable land in his own Scandinavia.

Why, then, did French-Canadian agriculture, despite the warm official encouragement given to it, make such relatively meager progress? There are several reasons for its backwardness. The long winters, which developed in the habitant an inveterate disposition to idleness, afford the clue to one of them. A general aversion to unremitting manual toil was one of the colony's besetting sins. Notwithstanding the small per capita acreage, accordingly, there was a continual complaint that not enough labor could be had to work the farms. Women and children were pressed into service in the busy seasons. Yet the colony abounded in idle men, and mendicancy at one time assumed such proportions as to require the enforcement of stringent penalties. The authorities were partly to blame for the development of this trait, for upon the slightest excuse they took the habitant from his daily routine and set him to help with warlike expeditions against the Indians and the English, or called him to build roads or to repair the fortifications. And the lure of the fur trade, which drew the most vigorous young men of the land off the farms into the forest, was another obstacle to the growth of yeomanry. Moreover, the curious and inconvenient shape of the farms, most of them mere ribbons of land, with a narrow frontage and disproportionate depth, handicapped all efforts to cultivate the fields in an intelligent way. Finally, there was the general poverty of the people. With a large family to support, for families of ten to fifteen children were not uncommon, it was hard for the settler to make both ends meet from the annual yield of a few *arpents*, however fertile. The habitant, therefore, took the shortest cut to everything, getting what he could out of his land in the quickest possible way with no reference to the ultimate improvement of the farm itself. If he ever managed to get a little money, he was likely to spend it at once and to become as impecunious as before. Such a propensity did not make for progress, for poverty begets slovenliness in all ages and among all races of men.

If anything like the industry and intelligence that was bestowed upon agriculture in the English colonies had been applied to the St. Lawrence valley, New France might have shipped far more wheat than beaver skins each year to Europe. But in this respect the colony never half realized the royal expectations. On the other hand, the attempt to make the land a rich grain-growing colony was far from being a flat failure. It was supporting its own population, and had a modest amount of grain each year for export to France or to the French West Indies. With peace it would soon have become a land of plenty, for the traveler who passed along the great river from Quebec to Montreal in the late autumn might see, as Kalm in his *Travels* tells us he saw, field upon field of waving grain extending from the shores inward as far as the eye could reach, broken only here and there by tracts of meadow and woodland. Here was at least the nucleus of a Golden West.

Of colonial industry, however, not as much can be said as of agriculture. Down to about 1663 it had given scarcely a single token of existence. The colony, until that date, manufactured nothing. Everything in the way of furnishings, utensils, apparel, and ornament was brought in the company's ships from France, and no one seemed to look upon this procedure as at all unusual. On the coming of Talon in 1665, however, the idea of fostering home industries in the colony took active shape. By persuasion and by promise of reward, the "Colbert of New France" interested the prominent citizens of Quebec in modest industrial enterprises of every sort.

But the outcome soon belied the intendant's airy hopes. It was easy enough to make a brave start in these things, especially with the aid of an initial subsidy from the treasury; but to keep the wheels of industry moving year after year without a subvention was an altogether different thing. A colony numbering less than ten thousand souls did not furnish an adequate market for the products of varied industries, and the high cost of transportation made it difficult to export manufactured wares to France or to the West Indies with any hope of profit. A change of tone, moreover, soon became noticeable in Colbert's dispatches with reference to industrial development. In 1665, when giving his first instructions to Talon, the minister had dilated upon his desire that Canada should become self-sustaining in the matter of clothing, shoes, and the simpler house-furnishings. But within a couple of years Colbert's mind seems to have taken a different shift, and we find him advising Talon that, after all, it might be better if the people of New France would devote their energies to agriculture and thus to raise enough grain wherewith to buy manufactured wares from France.   So, for one reason or another, the infant industries languished, and, after Talon was gone, they gradually dropped out of existence.

Another of Talon's ventures was to send prospectors in search of minerals.   The use of malleable copper by the Indians had been noted by the French for many years and various rumors concerning the source of supply had filtered through to Quebec.   Some of Talon's agents, including Jean Peré, went as far as the upper lakes, returning with samples of copper ore.   But the distance from Quebec was too great for profitable transportation and, although Père Dablon in 1670 sent down an accurate description of the great masses of ore in the Lake Superior region, many generations were to pass before any serious attempt could be made to develop this source of wealth.   Nearer at hand some titaniferous iron ore was discovered, at Baie St. Paul below Quebec, but it was not utilized, although on being tested it was found to be good in quality.   Then the intendant sent agents to verify reports as to rich coal deposits in Isle Royale (Cape Breton), and they returned with glowing accounts which subsequent industrial history has entirely justified.   Shipments of this coal were brought to Quebec for consumption.   A little later the intendant reported to Colbert that a vein of coal had been actually uncovered at the foot of the great rock which frowns upon the Lower Town at Quebec, adding that the vein could not be followed for fear of toppling over the Château which stood above. No one has ever since found any trace of Talon's coal deposit, and the geologists of today are quite certain that the intendant had more imagination than accuracy of statement or even of elementary mineralogical knowledge.

Above the settlement at Three Rivers some excellent deposits of bog iron ore were found in 1668, but it was not until five decades later that the first forges were established there. These were successfully operated throughout the remainder of the Old Régime, and much of the colony's iron came from them to supply the blacksmiths. From time to time rumors of other mineral discoveries came to the ears of the people. A find of lead was reported from the Gaspé peninsula, but an investigation proved it to be a hoax. Copper was actually found in a dozen places within the settled ranges of the colony, but not in paying quantities. Every one was always on the *qui vive* for a vein of gold or silver, but no part of New France ever gave the slightest hint of an El Dorado. Prospecting engaged the energies of many colonists in every generation, but most of those who thus spent their years at it got nothing but a princely dividend of chagrin.

Mention should also be made of the brewing industry which Talon set upon its feet during his brief intendancy but which, like all the rest of his schemes, did not long survive his departure. In establishing a brewery at Quebec the paternal intendant had two ends in mind: first, to reduce the large consumption of *eau-de-vie* by providing a cheaper and more wholesome substitute; and second, to furnish the farmers of the colony with a profitable home market for their grain. In 1771 Talon reported to the French authorities that the Quebec brewery was capable of turning out four thousand hogsheads of beer per annum, and thus of creating a demand for many thousand bushels of malt. Hops were also needed and were expensive when brought from France, so that the people were encouraged to grow hop-vines in the colony. But even with grain and hops at hand, the brewing industry did not thrive, and before many years Talon's enterprise closed its doors. The building was finally remodeled and became the headquarters of the later intendants.

Flour-making and lumbering were the two industries which made most consistent progress in the colony. Flour-mills were established both in and near Quebec at an early date, and in course of time there were scores of them scattered throughout the colony, most of them built and operated as *banal* mills by the seigneurs. The majority were windmills after the Dutch fashion, but some were water-driven. On the whole, they were not very efficient and turned out flour of such indifferent grade that the bakers of Quebec complained loudly on more than one occasion. In response to a request from the intendant, the King sent out some fanning-mills which were distributed to various seigneuries, but even this benefaction did not seem to make any great improvement in the quality of the product. Yet in some years the colony had flour of sufficiently good quality for export, and sent small cargoes both to France and to the French West Indies.

The sawing of lumber was carried on in various parts of the colony, particularly at Malbaie and at Baie St. Paul. Beam-timbers, planks, staves, and shingles were made in large quantities both for use in the colony and for export to France, where the timbers and planks were in demand at the

royal shipyards. Wherever lands were granted
by the Crown, a provision was inserted in the
title-deed reserving all oak timber and all pine
of various species suitable for mastings. Though
such timber was not to be cut without official
permission, the people did not always respect this
reservation. Yet the quantity of timber shipped
to France was very large, and next to furs it formed
the leading item in the cargoes of outgoing ships.
For staves there was a good market at Quebec
where barrels were being made for the packing of
salted fish and eels.

The various handicrafts or small industries,
such as blacksmithing, cabinet-making, pottery,
brick-making, were regulated quite as strictly in
Canada as in France. The artisans of the towns
were organized into *jurés* or guilds, and elected a
master for each trade. These masters were
responsible to the civil authorities for the proper
quality of the work done and for the observance of
all the regulations which were promulgated by the
intendant or the council from time to time.

This relative proficiency in home industry
accounts in part for the tardy progress of the colony in the matter of large industrial establishments. But there were other handicaps. For

one thing, the Paris authorities were not anxious to see the colony become industrially self-sustaining. Colbert in his earliest instructions to Talon wrote as though this were the royal policy, but no other minister ever hinted at such a desire. Rather it was thought best that the colony should confine itself to the production of raw materials, leaving it to France to supply manufactured wares in return. The mercantilist doctrine that a colony existed for the benefit of the mother country was gospel at Fontainebleau. Even Montcalm, a man of liberal inclinations, expressed this idea with undiminished vigor in a day when its evil results must have been apparent to the naked eye. "Let us beware," he wrote, "how we allow the establishment of industries in Canada or she will become proud and mutinous like the English colonies. So long as France is a nursery to Canada, let not the Canadians be allowed to trade but kept to their laborious life and military services."

The exclusion of the Huguenots from Canada was another industrial misfortune. A few Huguenot artisans came to Quebec from Rochelle at an early date, and had they been welcomed, more would soon have followed. But they were promptly deported. From an economic standpoint this was an unfortunate policy. The Huguenots were resourceful workmen, skilled in many trades. They would have supplied the colony with a vigorous and enterprising stock. But the interests of orthodoxy in religion were paramount with the authorities, and they kept from Canada the one class of settlers which most desired to come. Many of those same Huguenots went to England, and every student of economic history knows how greatly they contributed to the upbuilding of England's later supremacy in the textile and related industries.

If we turn to the field of commerce, the spirit of restriction appears as prominently as in the domain of industry. The Company of One Hundred Associates, during its thirty years of control, allowed no one to proceed to Quebec except on its own vessels, and nothing could be imported except through its storehouses. Its successor, the Company of the West Indies, which dominated colonial commerce from 1664 to 1669, was not a whit more liberal. Even under the system of royal government, the consistent keynotes of commercial policy were regulation, paternalism, and monopoly.

This is in no sense surprising. Spain had

first given to the world this policy of commercial constraint and the great enrichment of the Spanish monarchy was everywhere held to be its outcome. France, by reason of her similar political and administrative system, found it easy to drift into the wake of the Spanish example. The official classes in England and Holland would fain have had these countries do likewise, but private initiative and enterprise proved too strong in the end. As for New France, there were spells during which the grip of the trading monopolies relaxed, but these lucid intervals were never very long. When the Company of the West Indies became bankrupt in 1669, the trade between New France and Old was ostensibly thrown open to the traders of both countries, and for the moment this freedom gave Colbert and his Canadian apostle, Talon, an opportunity to carry out their ideas of commercial upbuilding.

The great minister had as his ideal the creation of a huge fleet of merchant vessels, built and operated by Frenchmen, which would ply to all quarters of the globe, bringing raw products to France and taking manufactured wares in return. It was under the inspiration of this ideal that Talon built at Quebec a small vessel and, having freighted it with lumber, fish, corn, and dried pease, sent it off to the French West Indies. After taking on board a cargo of sugar, the vessel was then to proceed to France and, exchanging the sugar for goods which were needed in the regions of the St. Lawrence, it was to return to Quebec. The intendant's plans for this triangular trade were well conceived, and in a general way they aimed at just what the English colonies along the Atlantic seaboard were beginning to do at the time. The keels of other ships were being laid at Quebec and the officials were dreaming of great maritime achievements. But as usual the enterprise never got beyond the sailing of the first vessel, for its voyage did not yield a profit.

The ostensible throwing-open of the colonial trade, moreover, did not actually change to any great extent the old system of paternalism and monopoly. Commercial companies no longer controlled the channels of transportation, it is true, but the royal government was not minded to let everything take its own course. So the trade was taxed for the benefit of the royal treasury, and the privilege of collecting the taxes, according to the custom of the old régime, was farmed out. All the commerce of the colony, imports and exports, had to pass through the hands of these farmers-of-the-revenue who levied ten per cent on all goods coming and kept for the royal treasury one-quarter of the price fixed for all skins exported. Traders as a rule were not permitted to ship their furs directly to France. They turned them in to farmers-of-the-revenue at Quebec, where they received the price as fixed by ordinance, less one-quarter. This price they usually took in bills of exchange on Paris which they handed over to the colonial merchants in payment for goods, and which the merchants in turn sent home to France to pay for new stocks. Nor were the authorities content with the mere fixing of prices. By ordinance they also set the rate of profit which traders should have upon all imported wares brought into the colony. This rate of profit was fixed at sixty-five per cent, but the traders had no compunction in going above it whenever they saw an opportunity which was not likely to be discovered. As far as the forest trade was concerned, the regulation was, of course, absurd.

Every year, about the beginning of May, the first ships left France for the St. Lawrence with general cargoes consisting of goods for the colonists themselves and for the Indians, as well as large quantities of brandy. When they arrived at Quebec, the vessels were met by the merchants of the town and by those who had come from Three Rivers and Montreal. For a fortnight lively trading took place. Then the goods which had been bought by the merchants of Montreal and Three Rivers were loaded upon small barques and brought to these towns to be in readiness for the annual fairs when the *coureurs-de-bois* and their Indians came down to trade in the late summer. As for the vessels which had come from France, these were either loaded with timber or furs and set off directly home again, or else they departed light to Cape Breton and took cargoes of coal for the French West Indies, where the refining of sugar occasioned a demand for fuel. The last ships left in November, and for seven months the colony was cut off from Europe.

Trade at Quebec, while technically open to any one who would pay the duties and observe the regulations as to rates of profit, was actually in the hands of a few merchants who had large warehouses and who took the greater part of what the ships brought in. These men were, in turn, affiliated more or less closely with the great trading houses which sent goods from Rouen or

Rochelle, so that the monopoly was nearly as iron-clad as when commercial companies were in control. When an outsider broke into the charmed circle, as happened occasionally, there was usually some way of hustling him out again by means either fair or foul. The monopolists made large profits, and many of them, after they had accumulated a fortune, went home to France. "I have known twenty of these pedlars," quoth La Hontan, "that had not above a thousand crowns stock when I arrived at Quebec in the year 1683 and when I left that place had got to the tune of twelve thousand crowns."

Glancing over the whole course of agriculture, industry, and commerce in New France from the time when Champlain built his little post at the foot of Cape Diamond until the day when the fleur-de-lis fluttered down from the heights above, the historian finds that there is one word which sums up the chief cause of the colony's economic weakness. That word is "paternalism." The Administration tried to take the place of Providence. It was as omnipresent and its ways were as inscrutable. Like as a father chasteneth his children, so the King and his officials felt it their duty to chasten every show of private initiative which did not direct itself along the grooves that they had marked out for the colony to follow. By trying to order everything they eventually succeeded in ordering nothing aright.

CHAPTER XI

In New France there were no privileged orders.
This, indeed, was the most marked difference
between the social organization of the home land
and that of the colony. There were social distinc-
tions in Canada, to be sure, but the boundaries
between different elements of the population were
not rigid; there were no privileges based upon the
laws of the land, and no impenetrable barrier separated one class from another. Men could rise by
their own efforts or come down through their own
defaults; their places in the community were not
determined for them by the accident of birth as
was the case in the older land. Some of the most
successful figures in the public and business affairs
of New France, some of the social leaders, some of
those who attained the highest rank in the *noblesse*,
came of relatively humble parentage.

In France of the sixteenth and seventeenth

centuries the chief officials of state, the seigneurs, the higher ecclesiastics, even the officers of the army and the marine, were always drawn from the nobility. In the colony this was very far from being the case. Some colonial officials and a few of the seigneurs were among the numerous *noblesse* of France before they came, and they of course retained their social rank in the new environment. Others were raised to this rank by the King, usually for distinguished services in the colony and on the recommendation of the governor or the intendant. But, even if taken all together, these men constituted a very small proportion of the people in New France. Even among the seigneurs the great majority of these landed gentlemen came from the ranks of the people, and not one in ten was a member of the *noblesse*. There was, therefore, a social solidarity, a spirit of fraternity, and a feeling of universal comradeship among them which was altogether lacking at home.

The pivot of social life in New France was the settlement at Quebec. This was the colonial capital, the seat of the governor and of the council, the only town in the colony large enough to have all the trappings and tinsel of a well-rounded social set. Here, too, came some of the seigneurs to spend the winter months. The royal officials, the officers of the garrison, the leading merchants, the judges, the notaries and a few other professional men — these with their families made up an élite which managed to echo, even if somewhat faintly, the pomp and glamor of Versailles. Quebec, from all accounts, was lively in the long winters. Its people, who were shut off from all intercourse with Europe for many months at a time, soon learned the art of providing for their own recreation and amusement. The knight-errant La Hontan speaks enthusiastically of the events in the life of this miniature society, of the dinners and dances, the salons and receptions, the intrigues, rivalries, and flirtations, all of which were well suited to his Bohemian tastes. But the clergy frowned upon this levity, of which they believed there was far too much. On one or two occasions they even laid a rigorous and restraining hand upon activities of which they disapproved, notably when the young officers of the Quebec garrison undertook an amateur performance of Molière's *Tartuffe* in 1694. At Montreal and Three Rivers, the two smaller towns of the colony, the social circle was more contracted and correspondingly less brilliant. The capital, indeed, had no rival.

Only a small part of the population, however, lived in the towns. At the beginning of the eighteenth century the census (1706) showed a total of 16,417, of whom less than 3000 were in the three chief settlements. The others were scattered along both banks of the St. Lawrence, but chiefly on the northern shore, with the houses grouped into *côtes* or little villages which almost touched elbows along the banks of the stream. In each of these hamlets the manor-house or home of the seigneur, although not a mansion by any means, was the focus of social life. Sometimes built of timber but more often of stone, with dimensions rarely exceeding twenty feet by forty, it was not much more pretentious than the homes of the more prosperous and thrifty among the seigneur's dependents. Its three or four spacious rooms were, however, more comfortably equipped with furniture which in many cases had been brought from France. Socially, the seigneur and his family did not stand apart from his neighbors. All went to the same church, took part in the same amusements upon days of festival, and not infrequently worked together at the common task of

clearing the lands. Sons and daughters of the
seigneurs often intermarried with those of habitants in the seigneury or of traders in the towns.
There was no social *impasse* such as existed in
France among the various elements in a community.

As for the habitants, the people who cleared
and cultivated the lands of the seigneuries, they
worked and lived and dressed as pioneers are
wont to do. Their homes were commonly built of
felled timber or of rough-hewn stone, solid, low,
stocky buildings, usually about twenty by forty
feet or thereabouts in size, with a single doorway
and very few windows. The roofs were steep-
pitched, with a dormer window or two thrust out
on either side, the eaves projecting well over the
walls in such manner as to give the structures a
half-bungalow appearance. With almost religious
punctuality the habitants whitewashed the outside of their walls every spring, so that from the
river the country houses looked trim and neat at
all seasons. Between the river and the uplands
ran the roadway, close to which the habitants set
their conspicuous dwellings with only in rare
cases a grass plot or shade tree at the door. In
winter they bore the full blast of the winds that

drove across the expanse of frozen stream in front of them; in summer the hot sun blazed relentlessly upon the low roofs. As each house stood but a few rods from its neighbor on either side, the colony thus took on the appearance of one long, straggling, village street. The habitant liked to be near his fellows, partly for his own safety against marauding Indians, but chiefly because the colony was at best a lonely place in the long cold season when there was little for any one to do.

Behind each house was a small addition used as a storeroom. Not far away were the barn and the stable, built always of untrimmed logs, the intervening chinks securely filled with clay or mortar. There was also a root-house, half-sunk in the ground or burrowed into the slope of a hill, where the habitant kept his potatoes and vegetables secure from the frost through the winter. Most of the habitants likewise had their own bake-ovens, set a convenient distance behind the house and rising four or five feet from the ground. These they built roughly of boulders and plastered with clay. With an abundance of wood from the virgin forests they would build a roaring fire in these ovens and finish the whole week's baking at one time. The habitant would often enclose a small plot of ground surrounding the house and outbuildings with a fence of piled stones or split rails, and in one corner he would plant his kitchen-garden.

Within the dwelling-house there were usually two, and never more than three, rooms on the ground floor. The doorway opened into the great room of the house, parlor, dining-room, and kitchen combined. A "living" room it surely was! In the better houses, however, this room was divided, with the kitchen partitioned off from the rest. Most of the furnishings were the products of the colony and chiefly of the family's own workmanship. The floor was of hewn timber, rubbed and scrubbed to smoothness. A woolen rug or several of them, always of vivid hues, covered the greater part of it. There were the family dinner-table of hewn pine, chairs made of pine saplings with seats of rushes or woven underbark, and often in the corner a couch that would serve as an extra bed at night. Pictures of saints hung on the walls. sharing the space with a crucifix, but often having for ominous company the habitant's flint-lock and his powder-horn hanging from the beams. At one end of the room was the fireplace and hearth, the sole means of heating the place, and usually the only means of cooking as well. Around it hung the array of pots and pans, almost the only things in the house which the habitant and his family were not able to make for themselves. The lack of colonial industries had the advantage of throwing each home upon its own resources, and the people developed great versatility in the cruder arts of craftsmanship.

Upstairs, and reached by a ladder, was a loft or attic running the full area of the house, but so low that one could touch the rafters everywhere. Here the children, often a dozen or more of them, were stowed away at night on mattresses of straw or feathers laid along the floor. As the windows were securely fastened, even in the coldest weather this attic was warm, if not altogether hygienic. The love of fresh air in his dwelling was not among the habitant's virtues. Every one went to bed shortly after darkness fell upon the land, and all rose with the sun. Even visits and festivities were not at that time prolonged into the night as they are nowadays. Therein, however, New France did not differ from other lands. In the seventeenth century most of the world went to bed at nightfall because there was nothing else to do, and no easy or inexpensive artificial light. Candles were in use, to be sure, but a great many more of them were burned on the altars of the churches than in the homes of the people. For his reading, the habitant depended upon the priest, and for his writing, upon the notary.

Clothing was almost wholly made at home. It was warm and durable, as well as somewhat distinctive and picturesque. Every parish had spinning wheels and handlooms in some of its homes on which the women turned out the heavy druggets or *étoffes du pays* from which most of the men's clothing was made. A great fabric it was, this homespun, with nothing but wool in it, not attractive in pattern but able to stand no end of wear. It was fashioned for the habitant's use into roomy trousers and a long frock coat reaching to the knees which he tied around his waist with a belt of leather or of knitted yarn. The women also used this *étoffe* for skirts, but their waists and summer dresses were of calico, homemade as well. As for the children, most of them ran about in the summer months wearing next to nothing at all. A single garment without sleeves and reaching to the knees was all that covered their nakedness. For all ages and for both sexes there were furs in plenty for winter use. Beaver skins were cheap, in some years about as cheap as cloth. When properly treated they were soft and pliable, and easily made into clothes, caps, and mittens.

Most of the footwear was made at home, usually from deerhides. In winter every one wore the *bottes sauvages*, or oiled moccasins laced up halfway or more to the knees. They were proof against cold and were serviceable for use with snowshoes. Between them and his feet the habitant wore two or more pairs of heavy woolen socks made from coarse homespun yarn. In summer the women and children of the rural communities usually went barefoot so that the soles of their feet grew as tough as pigskin; the men sometimes did likewise, but more frequently they wore, in the fields or in the forest, clogs made of cowhide.

On the week-days of summer every one wore a straw hat which the women of the household spent part of each winter in plaiting. In cold weather the knitted *tuque* made in vivid colors was the great favorite. It was warm and picturesque. Each section of the colony had its own color; the habitants in the vicinity of Quebec wore blue *tuques*, while those around Montreal preferred red. The apparel of the people was thus in general adapted to the country, and it had a distinctiveness that has not yet altogether passed away.

On Sundays and on the numerous days of festival, however, the habitant and his family brought out their best. To Mass the men wore clothes of better texture and high beaver hats, the women appeared in their brighter plumage of dresses with ribbons and laces imported from France. Such finery was brought over in so large a quantity that more than one *mémoire* to the home government censured the "spirit of extravagance" of which this was one outward manifestation. In the towns the officials and the well-to-do merchants dressed elaborately on all occasions of ceremony, with scarlet cloaks and perukes, buckled slippers and silk stockings. In early Canada there was no austerity of garb such as we find in Puritan New England. New France on a *jour de fête* was a blaze of color.

As for his daily fare, the habitant was never badly off even in the years when harvests were poor. He had food that was more nourishing and more abundant than the French peasant had at home. Bread was made from both wheat and rye flour, the product of the seigneurial mills. Corn cakes were baked in Indian fashion from ground maize. Fat salted pork was a staple during the winter, and nearly every habitant laid away each autumn a smoked supply of eels from the river. Game of all sorts he could get with little trouble at any time, wild ducks and geese, partridges, for there were in those days no game laws to protect them. In the early winter, likewise, it was indeed a luckless habitant who could not also get a caribou or two for his larder. Following the Indian custom, the venison was smoked and hung on the kitchen beams, where it kept for months until needed. Salted or smoked fish had also to be provided for family use, since the usages of the Church required that meat should not be used upon numerous fast-days.

Vegetables of many varieties were grown in New France, where the warm, sandy, virgin soil of the St. Lawrence region was splendidly suited for this branch of husbandry. Peas were the great stand-by, and in the old days whole families were reared upon *soupe aux pois*, which was, and may even still be said to be, the national dish of the French Canadians. Beans, cucumbers, melons, and a dozen other products were also grown in the family gardens. There were potatoes, which the habitant called *patates* and not *pommes de terre*,

but they were almost a rarity until the closing days
of the Old Régime.   Wild fruits, chiefly raspberries,
blueberries, and wild grapes, grew in abundance
among the foothills and were gathered in great
quantities every summer.   There was not much
orchard fruit, although some seedling trees were
brought from France and had managed to become
acclimated.

On the whole, even in the humbler homes
there was no need for any one to go hungry.   The
daily fare of the people was not of great variety,
but it was nourishing, and there was plenty of it
save in rare instances.   More than one visitor to
the colony was impressed by the rude comfort
in which the people lived, even though they
made no pretense of being well-to-do.   "In New
France," wrote Charlevoix, "poverty is hidden
behind an air of comfort," while the gossipy La
Hontan was of the opinion that "the boors of these
seigneuries live with greater comfort than an
infinity of the gentlemen in France."   Occasionally, when the men were taken from the fields to
serve in the defense of the colony against the
English attacks, the harvests were small and
the people had to spend the ensuing winter on
short rations.   Yet, as the authorities assured

the King, they were "robust, vigorous, and able in time of need to live on little."

As for beverages, the habitant was inordinately fond of sour milk. Tea was scarce and costly. Brandy was imported in huge quantities, and not all this *eau-de-vie*, as some writers imagine, went into the Indian trade. The people themselves consumed most of it. Every parish in the colony had its grog-shop; in 1725 the King ordered that no parish should have more than two. Quebec had a dozen or more, and complaint was made that the people flocked to these resorts early in the morning, thus rendering themselves unfit for work during most of the day, and soon ruining their health into the bargain. There is no doubt that the people of New France were fond of the flagon, for not only the priests but the civil authorities complained of this failing. Idleness due to the numerous holidays and to the long winters combined with the tradition of hospitality to encourage this taste. The habitants were fond of visiting one another, and hospitality demanded on every such occasion the proffer of something to drink. On the other hand, the scenes of debauchery which a few chroniclers have described were not typical of the colony the year round. When the ships came in with their cargoes, there was a great indulgence in feasting and drink, and the excesses at this time were sure to impress the casual visitor. But when the fleet had weighed anchor and departed for France, there was a quick return to the former quietness and to a reasonable measure of sobriety.

Tobacco was used freely. "Every farmer," wrote Kalm, "plants a quantity of tobacco near his house because it is universally smoked. Boys of twelve years of age often run about with the pipe in their mouths." The women were smokers, too, but more commonly they used tobacco in the form of snuff. In those days, as in our own, this French-Canadian tobacco was strong stuff, cured in the sun till the leaves were black, and when smoked emitting an odor that scented the whole parish. The art of smoking a pipe was one of several profitless habits which the Frenchman lost little time in acquiring from his Indian friends.

This convivial temperament of the inhabitants of New France has been noted by more than one contemporary. The people did not spend all their energies and time at hard labor. From October, when the crops were in, until May, when the season of seedtime came again, there was, indeed, little hard work for them to do. Aside from the cutting of firewood and the few household chores the day was free, and the habitants therefore spent it in driving about and visiting neighbors, drinking and smoking, dancing and playing cards. Winter, accordingly, was the great social season in the country as well as in the town.

The chief festivities occurred at Michaelmas, Christmas, Easter, and May Day. Of these, the first and the last were closely connected with the seigneurial system. On Michaelmas the habitant came to pay the annual rental for his lands; on May Day he rendered the Maypole homage which has been already described. Christmas and Easter were the great festivals of the Church and as such were celebrated with religious fervor and solemnity. In addition, minor festivals, chiefly religious in character, were numerous, so much so that their frequency even in the months of cultivation was the subject of complaint by the civil authorities, who felt that these holidays took altogether too much time from labor. Sunday was a day not only of worship but of recreation. Clad in his best raiment, every one went to Mass, whatever the distance or the weather.

The parish church indeed was the emblem of village solidarity, for it gathered within its walls each Sunday morning all sexes and ages and ranks. The habitant did not separate his religion from his work or his amusements; the outward manifestations of his faith were not to his mind things of another world; the church and its priests were the center and soul of his little community. The whole countryside gathered about the church doors after the service while the *capitaine de la côte*, the local representative of the intendant, read the decrees that had been sent to him from the seats of the mighty at the Château de St. Louis. That duty over, there was a garrulous interchange of local gossip with a retailing of such news as had dribbled through from France. The crowd then melted away in groups to spend the rest of the day in games or dancing or in friendly visits of one family with another.

Especially popular among the young people of each parish were the *corvées récréatives*, or "bees" as we call them nowadays in our rural communities. There were the *épuchlette* or corn-husking, the *brayage* or flax-beating, and others of the same sort. The harvest-home or *grosse-gerbe*, celebrated when the last load had been brought

in from the fields, and the *Ignolée* or welcoming
of the New Year, were also occasions of goodwill,
noise, and revelry. Dancing was by all odds
the most popular pastime, and every parish had
its fiddler, who was quite as indispensable a factor
in the life of the village as either the smith or the
notary. Every wedding was the occasion for
terpsichorean festivities which lasted all day long.

The habitant liked to sing, especially when working with others in the woods or when on the march.
The voyageurs relieved the tedium of their long
journeys by breaking into song at intervals. But
the popular repertoire was limited to a few folk-
songs, most of them songs of Old France. They
were easy to learn, simple to sing, but sprightly and
melodious. Some of them have remained on the
lips and in the hearts of the French-Canadian
race for over two hundred years. Those who do
not know the *Claire fontaine* and *Ma boulë
roulant* have never known French Canada. The
forêtier of today still goes to the woods chanting
the *Malbrouck s'en va-t-en guerre* which his ancestors
caroled in the days of Blenheim and Malplaquet.
When the habitant sang, moreover, it was in
no pianissimo tones; he was lusty and cheerful
about giving vent to his buoyant spirits. And

his descendant of today has not lost that propensity.

The folklore of the old dominion, unlike the folk music, was extensive. Some of it came with the colonists from their Norman firesides, but more, perhaps, was the outcome of a superstitious popular imagination working in the new and strange environment of the wilderness. The habitant had a profound belief in the supernatural, and was prone to associate miraculous handiwork with every unusual event. He peopled the earth and the air, the woods and the rivulets, with spirits of diverse forms and varied motives. The red man's abounding superstition, likewise, had some influence upon the habitant's highstrung temperament. At any rate, New France was full of legends and weird tales. Every island, every cove in the river, had one or more associated with it. Most of these legends had some moral lessons attached to them: they were tales of disaster which came from disobeying the teachings of the Church or of miraculous escape from death or perdition due to the supernatural rewarding of righteousness. Taken together, they make up a wholesome and vigorous body of folklore, reflecting both the mystic temper of the colony and the religious fervor of its common life. A distinguished son of French Canada has with great industry gathered these legends together, a service for which posterity will be grateful.[1]

Various chroniclers have left us pen portraitures of the habitant as they saw him in the olden days. Charlevoix, La Hontan, Hocquart, and Peter Kalm, men of widely different tastes and aptitudes, all bear testimony to his vigor, stamina, and native-born vivacity. He was courteous and polite always, yet there was no flavor of servility in this most benign trait of character. It was bred in his bone and was fostered by the teachings of his church. Along with this went a *bonhomie* and a lightheartedness, a touch of personal vanity, with a liking for display and ostentation, which unhappily did not make for thrift. The habitant "enjoys what he has got," writes Charlevoix, "and often makes a display of what he has not got." He was also fond of honors, even minor ones, and plumed himself on the slightest recognition from official circles. Habitants who by years of hard labor had saved enough to buy some uncleared seigneury strutted about with the airs of genuine aristocrats while their wives, in the

[1] Sir J. M. Lemoine, *Legends of the St. Lawrence* (Quebec, 1878).

words of Governor Denonville, "essayed to play the fine lady." More than one intendant was amused by this broad streak of vanity in the colonial character. "Every one here," wrote Meulles, "begins by calling himself an esquire and ends by thinking himself a nobleman."

Yet despite this attempt to keep up appearances, the people were poor. Clearing the land was a slow process, and the cultivable area available for the support of each household was small. Early marriages were the rule, and families of a dozen or more children had to be supported from the produce of a few *arpents*. To maintain such a family as this every one had to work hard in the growing season, and even the women went to the fields in the harvest-time. One serious shortcoming of the habitant was his lack of steadfastness in labor. There was a roving strain in his Norman blood. He could not stay long at any one job; there was a restlessness in his temperament which would not down. He would leave his fields unploughed in order to go hunting or to turn a few *sous* in some small trading adventure. Unstable as water, he did not excel in tasks that required patience. But he could do a great many things after a fashion, and some that could be done quickly he did surprisingly well.

One racial characteristic which drew comment from observers of the day was the litigious disposition of the people. The habitant would have made lawsuits his chief diversion had he been permitted to do so. "If this propensity be not curbed," wrote the intendant Raudot, "there will soon be more lawsuits in this country than there are persons." The people were not quarrelsome in the ordinary sense, but they were very jealous each one of his private rights, and the opportunities for litigation over such matters seemed to provide themselves without end. Lands were given to settlers without accurate description of their boundaries; farms were unfenced and cattle wandered into neighboring fields; the notaries themselves were almost illiterate, and as a result scarcely a legal document in the colony was properly drawn. Nobody lacked pretexts for controversy. Idleness during the winter was also a contributing factor. But the Church and the civil authorities frowned upon this habit of rushing to court with every trivial complaint. *Curés* and seigneurs did what they could to have such difficulties settled amicably at home, and in a considerable measure they succeeded.

New France was born and nurtured in an atmosphere of religious devotion. To the habitant the Church was everything — his school, his counselor, his almsgiver, his newspaper, his philosopher of things present and of things to come. To him it was the source of all knowledge, experience, and inspiration, and to it he never faltered in ungrudging loyalty. The Church made the colony a spiritual unit and kept it so, undefiled by any taint of heresy. It furnished the one strong, well-disciplined organization that New France possessed, and its missionaries blazed the way for both yeoman and trader wherever they went.

Many traits of the race have been carried on to he present day without substantial change. The abitant of the old dominion was a voluble talker, a teller of great stories about his own feats of skill and endurance, his hair-raising escapes, or his astounding prowess with musket and fishing-line. Stories grew in terms of prodigious achievement as they passed from tongue to tongue, and the scant regard for anything approaching the truth in these matters became a national eccentricity. The habitant was boastful in all that concerned himself or his race; never did a people feel more firmly assured that it was the salt of the earth.   He was proud of his ancestry, and proud of his allegiance; and so are his descendants of today even though their allegiance has changed.

To speak of the habitants of New France as downtrodden or oppressed, dispirited or despairing, like the peasantry of the old land in the days before the great Revolution, as some historians have done, is to speak untruthfully.   These people were neither serfs nor peons.   The habitant, as Charlevoix puts it, "breathed from his birth the air of liberty"; he had his rights and he maintained them.   Shut off from the rest of the world, knowing only what the Church and civil government allowed him to know, he became provincial in his horizon and conservative in his habits of mind. The paternal policy of the authorities sapped his initiative and left him little scope for personal enterprise, so that he passed for being a dull fellow. Yet the annals of forest trade and Indian diplomacy prove that the New World possessed no sharper wits than his.   Beneath a somewhat ungainly exterior the yeoman and the trader of New France concealed qualities of cunning, tact, and quick judgment to a surprising degree.

These various types in the population of New France, officials, missionaries, seigneurs, voyageurs, habitants, were all the scions of a proud race, admirably fitted to form the rank and file in a great crusade. It was not their fault that France failed to dominate the Western Hemisphere.

BIBLIOGRAPHICAL NOTE

The foundation of France's first claim to territory in the New World is established in *The Voyages of Giovanni da Verrazzani, 1524–1528* by Lawrence W. Wroth (1970). An additional source is Pierre de Charlevoix's *Journal of a Voyage to North America,* in two volumes, translated and edited by I. P. Kellogg (1923, reprinted 1969).

Those interested in the background and destiny of New France remain indebted to Francis Parkman (1823–1893) whose works are particularly valuable including the following in many editions: *Pioneers of New France, Old Regime in Canada, Jesuits in North America, La Salle and the Discovery of the Great West, Count Frontenac,* and *Frontenac and New France under Louis XIV.*

In *The Chronicles of Canada* (1913–1916) titles especially recommended are *Dawn of Canadian History* and *Mariner of St. Malo* by Stephen Leacock; *Founder of New France* and *The Fighting Governor* by Charles W. Colby; *Seigneurs of Old France* and *Coureurs de Bois* by William B. Munro; *Great Intendant* by Thomas Chapais and *Jesuit Missions* by Thomas G. Marquis.

A good survey treatise on New France is *Canada*

Under Louis XIV, 1663–1701 (1964) by William J. Eccles in the *Canadian Centenary Series*. Also by Eccles are *The Canadian Frontier, 1534–1760* (1969) and *France in America* (1972), both of which contribute substantially to an appraisal of New France's past. Among the most useful studies is the monumental work by Gustave Lanctot in three volumes, *The History of Canada* (1963–65) which traces New France from its origins to the Treaty of Paris in 1763. Also of value is *An Introduction to New France* (1968) by Marcel Trudel.

The Pulitzer Prize historian Samuel Eliot Morison has written an excellent account of the founder of France in America in *Samuel de Champlain, Father of New France* (1972). Another useful biography is *Champlain, the Life of Fortitude* (1948) by Morris Bishop while the *Voyages of Samuel de Champlain, 1604–1618* (1907, reprinted 1959), edited by W. L. Grant, sheds further light on this intrepid explorer.

The greatest of New France's governors is the subject of William D. La Seur's biography *Count Frontenac* (1971) and also of La Seur's earlier work, *Frontenac, the Courtier Governor* (1959).

John F. McDermott is the editor of *The French in the Mississippi Valley* (1965), fourteen essays which give a carefully documented and fascinating picture of the discovery and exploration of the Louisiana territory. La Salle's last exploration and death are covered in Robert S. Weddle's *Wilderness Manhunt: The Spanish Search for La Salle* (1973).

A readable account of the Jesuits in New France and their relations with the Indians is *Jesuits and the Indian Wars of the Northwest* by Robert I. Burns (1966). The great Jesuit missionary and explorer is well limned in Joseph P. Donnelly's *Jacques Marquette: 1637–1675* (1968).

The Iroquois Indians have their historian in Charles M. Johnston, author of *Valley of the Six Nations* (1963).

The clash between England and France in the New World is traced (with particular reference to the English viewpoint) commencing with the first conflicts in *The Northern Colonial Frontier, 1607–1763* (1966) by Douglas E. Leach.

The Seigneural System in Early Canada (1966) is a scholarly work by Richard C. Harris. The cultural and social life of both peasants and the highly born in New France is well described in *Daily Life in Early Canada* (1968) by Raymond Douville and Jacques Casanova.

INDEX

Algonquins, The, act as guides to Champlain, 41; friendly to the French, 45

Anticosti, Island of, 19, 20

Arrêts of Marly (1711), 143

Belle Isle, 18, 19, 20

Bigot, François, 68

Brébeuf, Jean de, Jesuit missionary, 56

Brouage, birthplace of Champlain, 33

Cambrai, Peace of (1729), 15

Canada, *see* New France

Cap Rouge, Cartier winters at, 26; Roberval winters at, 28

Cartier, Jacques, sets out on first voyage of discovery, (1534), 16; a corsair, 16; former voyages, 17; reaches New World, 18; purpose of expedition, 19; returns home, 19; begins second voyage, 19–20; his ships, 20; winters at Stadacona, 21–23; learns of Great Lakes, 22; takes Indians to King, 23; account of voyage, 24; sails on third voyage from St. Malo (1541), 25; winters at Cap Rouge, 26; defies patron, Roberval, 27; personal characteristics, 29; later life, 29; death (1557), 29; bibliography, 229

Catalogne, Gedéon de, makes survey and maps of Quebec region (1712), 143–44; makes agricultural census, 184

Cataraqui (Kingston), fort established at, 85–86; La Salle receives grant of land at, 103

Chaleurs, Baie des, 18

Champlain, Samuel de, born at Brouage (1567), 33; sails with expedition of De Chastes (1603), 33; personal characteristics, 33–34; embarks as chief geographer (1604), 35; winters at St. Croix, 36–37; *Order de Bon Temps*, 38; returns to France, 39; sails again for the St. Lawrence (1608), 39; raid against the Iroquois, 41; seeks western passage to Cathay, 44; makes journeys into interior (1613 and 1616), 44–47; journals, 47; as viceroy's deputy, 48; surrenders to English, 51–52; returns to Quebec as representative of Company of One Hundred Associates, 52; death (1635), 53; appreciation of, 53–54

Champlain, Lake, 41

Chastes, Amyar, Sieur de, 32, 33, 34

Chauvin of Honfleur, 32

Church in New France, loyalty to, 113; Récollets, 115; Jesuits, 116 *et seq.;* aid to civil power, 127–28; revenues, 129–130; *see also* Jesuits

Colbert, Jean Baptiste, personal characteristics, 8; interest in